Greatly Blessed Highly Favoured Deeply Loved

Greatly Blessed
Highly Favoured
Deeply Loved

EILEEN MILLER

Greatly Blessed, Highly Favoured, Deeply Loved

Paperback: ISBN: 978-1-62020-980-6
eBook: ISBN: 978-1-62020-994-3

Printed in UK

Ambassador International
Emerald House
411 University Ridge, Suite B14
Greenville, SC 29601
www.ambassador-international.com

Ambassador Books and Media
The Mount
2 Woodstock Link
Belfast, BT6 8DD, Northern Ireland, UK
www.ambassadormedia.co.uk

Dedication

First and foremost I want to give thanks to almighty God who saved me and has kept me all these years. Without His guiding, leading and anointing the writing of this book would never have been accomplished. I give all the praise, honour and glory to the Lord of Lords and King of Kings.

I want to thank and dedicate this book to my darling husband, Ian who put up with the many hours I was not available and screened all telephone calls and visitors to give me time alone with God and to write. Your love and support has been unwavering and even though we are apart many weeks each year you are my encourager and motivator, never ever complaining but knowing I must be about my Father's business. The many cups of coffee you brought to me and many meals you lovingly made to free-up more time for me, thank you dear so very much. Ian, you are the very best husband a girl could have but more than this, you are my soul mate and best friend. May God bless you with many more healthy years.

Also to my daughter Sharon, her husband Noel, my granddaughter Katie and my son Derek you are simply the best. To my sisters Elizabeth and Dorothy and my dear brother George; God bless you each one and show you great favour for the way you have blessed me in multiple ways. Your support and love has carried me through both good times and difficult time.

To my partner in the ministry, Pastor Godfrey Mugolo in Uganda, who always upholds me before the throne and is a stalwart of the ministry. Thank you for everything you do for me but above all you do it for the Lord. I Pray a fresh anointing upon your life and more doors opening to preach the Word of God.

You each are a lily among the thorns. Song of Solomon 2:2

"Dear reader, it is my pleasure to introduce this great book to you and by the time you come to the end of it all, you will not be the same. As you read through this book, you will get to learn what it means to be Blessed, Favoured and Loved by your Creator which I know, will create space in your heart to trust God in all situations, commit to what God has called you for no matter what challenge.

Besides the self-proclaimed ministers, Eileen Miller is a blessed teacher of the word, favoured by God and loved by men wherever she has been doing the work of ministry. I have travelled with her to different places and in different countries in Africa and I have witnessed to this. So it is not by mistake that she entitled this book Greatly Blessed, Highly Favoured and Deeply Loved. God bless you as you embrace this book."

Pastor Godfrey Mugolo
Good News For All Global Ministires – Uganda

Contents

"I have known Eileen Miller for many years now and I have found her to be totally committed to the Lord. This book tells her story. How as a young girl brought up in a Christian household, she gave her life to Jesus at the young age of 13 years. Her walk with Jesus has not always been easy but her faith has always been firm. Through the lows of critical illnesses, she stood strong and her Lord brought her through those episodes in her life. To the call for her to enter the mission field in places such as Kenya, Uganda, Rwanda etc. As you read this book you will see that Eileen could not have chosen a better title, as she has been: Greatly Blessed, Highly Favoured and Deeply Loved."

Pastor Alan Patton

Church of God, Larne, Northern Ireland

"As you read of Eileen's journey I am certain that you will conclude that she is of that rare category of saints who dare to step beyond the boundaries of confined religious routine into the midstream of supernatural supply and miraculous manifestation. Read, enjoy, be blessed and challenged."

Evangelist Herbert Moody

Souls Outreach Association, Durban, South Africa

Foreword

In taking up Eileen Miller's 'travelogue' I am quickly made aware of her journey through life with snapshots and memories of her road travelled. The rich experiences gathered along the way are thoughtfully woven into her life's tapestry, but equally, I catch a sense of her road ahead and the anticipation of it. Her desire that others may join within this journey as well prepared sojourners is palpable. She holds nothing back in this telling testimonial to the power of God breaking forth when at her lowest point in life.

Be prepared to have your heart touched by her honesty and warm style of story-telling inscribed in an account packing all the punch of a challenging sermon delivered by a seasoned preacher and teacher. This is not the handwriting of a case-hardened servant of God, rather it is the gracious hand of God upon a bruised follower of Christ. Those who have endured life's knocks will find enlightenment within these pages; those unable to accept God's will for them will discover grace amidst their personal trials; those who have lost their way will find signposts saying, *"This is the way, walk ye in it."* (Isaiah 30:21) and those who no longer know what to believe, or even what is their true identity and purpose in life, will be blown away by a God with a staggering message for wearied travellers... *"For I know the thoughts that I think toward you, saith the LORD, thoughts of peace, and not of evil, to give you an expected end."* (Jeremiah 29:11)

"Eileen opens to the reader the mystery of God's will and purpose to both believer and sceptic. I am reminded of a text from Ecclesiastes 3:11 where the Preacher lays claim that "*He hath made every thing beautiful in his time…*" The beauty spoken of here is not that beheld by the human eye but that which is seen from the perspective of an almighty Father who is ever eager to give the best of gifts to His children (Matthew 7:9-11).

Eileen draws from her own experiences of a desperately forlorn future. Her healing testimony is not so much about what God has done for her but what God intends to do through her. In a 'me-first' society she will lift eyes to appreciate the higher perspective of God's plan in reaching out to all nations. Her book is masterful in its simplicity. It presents the Gospel openly and honestly in a manner that will appeal to all, from paupers to princes. It is a warm passionate yet compassionate read which will humble the proud and raise the lowly in spirit. It is what can only be described as a 'timely word for all seasons of life' and a reminder that "… *without faith it is impossible to please Him…*" (Hebrews 11:6). If it is true that 'you cannot put a good man down' then it is even truer that 'you cannot put a good book down', of which this book is most certainly true!"

Rev Jim Neil,
United Free Church of Scotland,
September 2019

What a title, what a book. This is Eileen Miller's first book, but as you read through the pages, you are taken on a journey, her journey, serving God in her own way.

As you join Eileen on this journey that started more than twenty years ago, you will notice as you read through this book, that you may well discover in part or in full that you have yourself been on just such a journey. I know as I was reading through this book, that so much of what Eileen Miller describes, has reflected my own walk.

God has a task and a plan for every Christian that is willing to wait on Him and do as He dictates. I have taken a plan which I believed was from God and run with it only to fall flat on my face because it was not the right time to run with the plan. You will read that Eileen Miller also had such thoughts, and how the Lord got her attention. He does get her attention, but she had to suffer from a stroke and be in a place to totally have to rely on God, and God alone.

She has now come to a place where she can no longer run away and hide behind her very prestigious job. She had to realise that God now has her full attention. For the rest of her journey, you will have to read through this book. As you do so why not stop at the points along Eileen's journey, that you recognise as a point on your own journey, why not pause to speak to God and apologise for being in the wrong place and in the wrong frame of mind, then wait for God and for Him to respond back to you. When you get to the end of Eileen Miller's journey, plan a time to take out of your schedule, to take yourself to a quiet place, and speak to God, tell Him that you are sorry, tell Him that you are now in a place to hear what His plans are for your life.

Once you have reached this point not only with the book but also on your journey with God, do a friend a favour and recommend that they too get their selves a copy of this book. It may only be Eileen Miller's first step as an author, but this book was twenty years in the making. As her journey continues, be on the lookout for further instalments from this Internationally known Evangelist, Bible Teacher and now a published author.

In His Service,

William K. Mackie

Rev Dr William K Mackie (Third Millennium Covenanters)

"There is no knowing what the Lord can do with a life that has been surrendered to Him. Only He knows the potential and the purpose He has placed in that individual. Sometimes He allows problems and trials in order to develop and bring to fruition that which He has determined to be there. "Greatly Blessed, Highly Favoured and Deeply Loved", tells one such story of a life devoted to the LORD and the working of His wisdom. Eileen Miller saved at an early age and shaped by the Almighty hands of the Potter has proved the grace, love, strength, and the absolute commitment of the LORD to those whom He calls to fulfill His purposes, whether at home or on the mission fields of the world."

Pastor Denver Michael

Elim Pentecostal Church, Cullybackey, Northern Ireland

Waiting for God

Have you ever been lying in bed at night trying to get to sleep, and sleep would not come? It is not long before the dawning of the new day and each hour of the clock you watch. All you desire is for time to pass that you may arise and commence a new day. 'Why can't this waiting be over?', you ask. You yearn for the dark hours of the night to swiftly go by and the morning to break on a new day. Every five minutes stretches out like an hour.

The Psalmist David says this is how he was waiting for God. He waits and he waits, with longing in his heart and soul, a long arduous waiting was happening on God to answer.

> "*I wait for the LORD, my soul doth wait, and in his word do I hope. My soul waiteth for the Lord more than they that watch for the morning: I say, more than they that watch for the morning.*" Psalm 130:5-6

> "*But thou, when thou prayest, enter into thy closet, and when thou hast shut thy door, pray to thy Father which is in secret; and thy Father which seeth in secret shall reward thee openly.*" Matthew 6:6

I have my own secret place where I withdraw to. That place is my study upstairs which is perfect for me as it is away from all the activity of the home and prohibits distractions.

Another secret place for me is in a local beauty area. On a good summer's day I rise and go for a walk along the river until I reach a particular tree where I can sit and be alone with God. The ripple of the water as it flows and the singing of the birds helps my mind to focus on the Creator as well as enjoying His creation.

How often do we go into the secret place with good intentions to wait on God but if He does not speak quickly, we get up and leave? Our thinking is possibly that it is wasting time to wait when we have so much else to do and accomplish. But, waiting on God is never a waste of time. Let me share with you why I am confident in stating this.

It was the spiritual desire for the Psalmist to wait for God. Note what he says: "*more than they that watch for the morning.*" And "*I say.*"

What David is really saying is, "Do you hear me? Are you listening to me? Take note! I am waiting for God. I want Him to come but I must wait for God's time — not my time. Oh Lord, come but as I wait, I dwell on your Word and claim your promises."

One of these important promises for me is found in Jeremiah 33:3, "*Call unto me, and I will answer thee, and shew thee great and mighty things, which thou knowest not.*" "*Call unto me and I will answer thee*" is a precious promise that God gave me when He called me into service. When I pray, I pray with confidence knowing that God will answer.

Sometimes as a Christian our walk is like that of a romantic couple. When they fall in love, and you cannot separate them, we call them 'sticking plasters', that which sticks together. Sometimes, they will even sit and look at each other, not even talking, just admiring. Words are not necessary; just being close in each other's company is suffice. Then as we get older or, dare I say, more familiar with the other person, it's like, "Why are you not talking to me?" comes out of our mouth and it may not be served in love. I am sure you know exactly what I mean.

Have you ever considered for the slightest moment that God is still in love with us, still admiring us, still gazing like a lover who just wants to spend time with us, and yet for us, it's like 'hurry up, answer my questions, speak to me and let me be on my way again!'

Are we like this, child of God? I know concerning myself in the past I have often been too busy. This to do, that place to go, someone to visit, the phone ringing, people messaging and cutting in on my time. And yet the very one who died for me, if I do not have time for Him to speak to me how then may I demonstrate my love for Him? We must ask ourselves why?

Remember 'intentions' are not the same as 'actions.'

How many of us at some time have gone past our dinner time and our stomach growls with hunger and then we create a dinner by making it or purchasing it. What is the difference between 'intending to eat it' or 'actually eating it?' The difference is intentions can cause you to die of hunger if you did not take action and eat. Likewise, intentions can cause you to miss divine opportunities but action under God will grasp every opportunity in God.

In Psalm 40:1 David says to us that, *"I waited patiently for the LORD."*

What does God have to do to get your attention and mine for us to know how important it is to wait upon Him? Could it be something very dramatic?

I recall back in April 2004 when God really got my attention by calling me aside. It is something I am not proud of, but God turned it around for His glory and blessings, not only to me but to others. Yes, God had given me many opportunities to come aside for a time with Him, but I ignored the prompting of the Holy Spirit and carried on as normal, each day following another. That still small voice was speaking gently but Eileen chose to ignore it, and this was to my peril. My career was too important and was occupying all of my time. It was a great career, the envy of many people, and it also commanded a very high salary, but God was not getting first place in my life as He did when I first was saved at 13 years of age. I was reading my Bible and praying but there was no time for an intimate walk with God. I was too busy pursuing my career and keeping on top of events around the world politically, financially, and industrially.

My position at the head of International Trade for the United Kingdom and Ireland meant I worked directly with the international divisions of the main financial institutions. Then there was the legal side to keep on top of, so I delivered seminars for Chambers of Commerce on European law and international legal requirements all over the UK. There was also the need for me to keep training manuals updated as things changed daily in a volatile world. This brought me into contact with the Embassies from around the globe as the legal documents for the movement of goods often had to go to the Embassy of the country involved. I got to understand the Arab nations and their take on the rest of the world — especially what their attitude was and still is to Israel. I loved the buss of it, and I loved knowing what was happening around the world before it was announced on the world scene.

When God could not get me to stop and listen by gentle nudging and whispering, He had to do something more drastic. Friend, be careful for God will do whatever it takes to get you to stop and turn around to Him. He did it in biblical times and times past and He still does it today.

Remember Jonah, one of the Minor Prophets, in the Old Testament? The story is found in the book of Jonah, chapters 1-2.

Jonah is the name given in the Hebrew Bible to a prophet of the Northern Kingdom of Israel around the 8th century BC. The Book opens with God speaking to Jonah, son of Amittai, commanding him to preach repentance to the city of Nineveh. He is called upon by God to travel to Nineveh and warn its residents to repent of their sins. We know from Jonah's account that he was hearing from God but was totally disobedient to God's command. He found the order unbearable. Not only was Nineveh known for its wickedness, but it was also the capital of the Assyrian empire, one of Israel's fiercest enemies. Jonah, a stubborn fellow, did just the opposite of what he was told.

He went down to the seaport of Joppa and booked passage on a ship to Tarshish, heading directly away from Nineveh. The Bible tells us in Jonah 1:3 that he, "*rose up to flee unto Tarshish from the presence of the Lord.*" Effectively he ran away from the Lord. A lesson you and I need to know and learn is that you cannot run away from God nor can you or I outrun God.

In response to him running away, God sent a violent storm to stop him, which threatened to break the ship to pieces. The terrified crew cast lots, determining that Jonah was responsible for the storm. Jonah told them to throw him overboard.

The reason he sought to be thrown off the boat was what was manifesting on the inside of him — rejection. Rejection will seek to self-harm oneself to the point, those who are with you; one will seek for them to cast you off. Jonah knowing that he was now outside the will of God was seeking to further put himself outside God's will. Did he not realise…

> *"Whither shall I go from thy spirit? or whither shall I flee from thy presence? If I ascend up into heaven, thou art there: if I make my bed in hell, behold, thou art there. If I take the wings of the morning, and dwell in the uttermost parts of the sea; Even there shall thy hand lead me, and thy right hand shall hold me. If I say, Surely the darkness shall cover me; even the night shall be light about me. Yea, the darkness hideth not from thee; but the night shineth as the day: the darkness and the light are both alike to thee."* Psalm 139:7-12

In seeking to save Jonah, they tried rowing to shore, but the waves became even higher. Afraid of God, the sailors finally tossed Jonah into the sea, and the water immediately grew calm. The crew made a sacrifice to God, swearing vows to him.

While Jonah was likely thinking his life was now over, God had sent a heavenly postal service wrapped up in a great fish and Jonah dropped right into its letterbox. With all the filth and revolting smell and food that would have been within the belly of the whale, Jonah must have felt sick and at his wit's end, but Jonah repented and cried out to God in prayer, ending with the eerily prophetic statement, *"I will pay that that I have vowed. Salvation is of the LORD."* Jonah 2:9

After three days of living in the stench of the giant fish, God commanded the whale to let Jonah go, and it vomited the prophet onto dry land. How miraculous was that? Jonah quickly learned you can't run away from God.

If we could only grasp that quick obedience to Jesus who is Life, brings life and life more abundant. And Jonah, slow to obedience, responds, moves into obedience by obeying God and walks into Nineveh proclaiming that in 40 days the city would be destroyed. Surprisingly, the Ninevites believed Jonah's message and repented, wearing sackcloth and covering themselves in ashes. God had compassion on them and did not destroy them. Jonah should have been thrilled at the response of his preaching and souls turning to God in their thousands. But no! Jonah was angry that God spared Israel's enemies. When Jonah left the city and sat down to rest God provided a 'gourd' or vine to shelter him from the heat of the sun. This pleased Jonah but the next day, God sent a worm to kill the vine making it wither up. Jonah grew faint in the hot sun and started complaining to God again. God was angry with him for having more concern for the vine than he had for 120,000 lost people.

While many of us may not be out on a sea for the Lord to send a fish to swallow us up. Sometimes it is not about the 'fish', it is what the fish could be in our life.

We see in this story…

1. God commands everything in His Creation, from the weather to a whale, to carry out His plan.
2. God is in control.
3. God can provide a supernatural means of rescue when His child is in trouble.

The story shows Jonah was hearing but not obeying, as he was running away from God.

As Scripture states, *"He that hath an ear, let him hear..."* Revelation 3:6

Most people have a set of ears to hear what is going on around us in the natural world. But when we are born-again, we are given a spiritual sense to hear what is now going on around us in the Spirit. But for many, because we have been so tuned into our natural senses, we find it difficult to tune into our spiritual senses.

When Revelation states, *"He that has ears to hear, let him hear..."* This is not referring to natural ears but having a spiritual sense as onto what our ears do. Listen carefully, many times in the Bible Jesus was hearing in the Spirit while His disciples were hearing in the natural. The word *'hear'* does not just refer to as in to listen, but to hearken as to obey. If you take anything out of this chapter, take this… when God is speaking to you, it is because He knows something we do not know or we're not fully aware of. Are you like Jonah, listening but not hearing? It is the 'hearing' that manifests the 'doing' of the will of God in our life.

There was an area in my life where I had sensed God speaking to me regarding a direction on my life and ministry. Like Jonah, I was about to find out, God's way is the best way. I, too, had tried to run away and hide from God.

Disobedience to God's Call

God had called me into full-time work in 1990 and I was obedient to the call, but in 1993 after suffering a dreadful hurt while in church ministry, that nearly destroyed me mentally as well as physically, I chose to leave the work of God and pursue my career. Not a wise move. I did not go to the secret place and wait patiently on the Lord but prayed without waiting at all. Over the following years, I took the attitude that I would never allow myself to be in a place to be hurt by a church or the people of a church ever again.

God had to deal severely with me to get me to stop running away. It is not God's pleasure to chastise His children but when He does, He always does it out of great love. **My idol was my career, it was my number one.** In Exodus 20:3 the first commandment reads, "*Thou shalt have no other gods before me.*" Bringing this into everyday language, what God is saying here, any job, person, career, possessions, anything at all that I put before God is another god. Let me just add a few more… that idol can be our church, our pastor, our ministry. Anything that we look up to and depend more on, than our Source — God!

As for me, there were many idols. My career was so important to me and taking up so much time that it was one of my idols if not my god. I tried to reconcile this by telling myself I was still attending church and reading my Bible.

Another idol I had was the perks I enjoyed and did not want to relinquish; for example, a good car that could be regarded as a status symbol and dressing in a suit and high heel shoes carrying a briefcase. My word carried great authority and my signature would mean a company's goods could be released into another country. If the choice came from attending the prayer meeting or giving a talk to company executives, I would choose the latter. Then it became that the ministry for me was nothing godly but carrying out the duties my professional career dictated. Even though I was living a 'clean' life and kept my high moral standards, even though temptations came many times, and in many ways, I would be offered bribes for business transactions to be passed. Men would think they could buy me with gifts or with less flattering invitations, but I never ever allowed this to happen as God gave me the strength to reject immoral business actions. They all knew where I stood, for I made it clear that it was honest business, or I walked away. Despite my moral stance it is clear to see how I was breaking the first commandment and that could not be allowed to continue.

It was springtime; my favourite time of year and all seemed to be so good. I flew home on a Friday evening and as I came off the plane and walked into the baggage reclaim all I could think of was having a lovely weekend with the love of my life, my husband, Ian, and my family, daughter, Sharon, and son, Derek. When I was away from home, I would always miss Ian very much though we talked every evening on the phone from my hotel room. At that time, we were enjoying 32 years of marriage. My children are very precious to me and time spent with them is always very valuable. I love just sitting with them and talking about whatever comes to mind. At that time Sharon was working hard in one of the banks and trying to save money for the future. Derek was home from England after having graduated in the year 2000. He was working just outside Belfast but still living at home. We had a nice evening together and I went to bed happy and well. However, in the morning it was a different story. My husband found me lying in bed unresponsive. The doctor was called, and an ambulance, and I was rushed to the hospital. It was confirmed that I had suffered a major stroke. What a shock for everyone, I had lost my ability to swallow, my speech was gone, and I was totally paralysed down the right side. When I gained consciousness again the family soon realised, I was alive, but I was a total mess. So, what now and where do we go from here?

I thank God that my thinking was not affected and as I lay there, I knew there was only one thing I could do and that was to surrender totally to God and trust Him in and through all things. When you are lying on your back there is only one way to look and that is up to God Himself. I cried unto God and asked Him to heal me. I cried and agonised in prayer, "Lord, if you will give me back my speech and give me movement and strength again in my body, I will forget my career and I will serve you the rest of my life." This was a sincere prayer cried from the depth of the pit I was in. There was no one who could help me, and I knew it would take a touch from the Master's hand. I repented completely of my disobedience and choosing to put my career first. How far had I gone and denied the pleading of the Lord? Repentance was the only way for me. I had gone from walking close with God; it was not God leaving me. Thank God He heard my cry and He was gracious unto me. This shows you the merciful and forgiving God and Father He is to His children even those who are disobedient.

There were many long days of despair and much crying. Lying in a hospital bed totally dependent on someone coming to attend to all my needs was not pleasant. The complete loss of dignity is one of the worst things a man or woman experiences. Also, to have the fluids I was to consume thickened so I would not choke was, for me, very unpleasant. My best description of this was like trying to take wallpaper paste; a bland taste and dreadful sticky texture. Adding coffee into this mixture, to flavour, did not make any difference rather, in my opinion, it was a waste of good coffee. I lay in bed and each day was so long and a repeat of the day before. Hope was fading fast that any improvement would come. I was an emotional wreck as well which did not help matters as this was contributing to mounting stress levels and I suffered further strokes over the period of months.

After many weeks the medical team, in the stroke unit caring for me, made the decision I should be moved to the geriatric unit of another hospital to live out the rest of my days. Again, I cried and cried. This was the unit where elderly patients suffering from severe dementia and such like illnesses were homed. I could not agree to such a move. Remember I had my full senses so could think clearly and was aware of the planning. I was mentally alert, but my body was not functioning as it should. What could I do and who could I go to that had clout to speak for me? The only one I could turn to was God and that is exactly what I did. I cried to God to overturn the decision and I kept reminding Him that I would serve Him diligently. Lying there on my back I continually went before the throne asking and claiming healing in the name of Jesus Christ.

I could claim healing because I knew the Scriptures and the doctrine of healing. Not only did I know them but more importantly I believed the Scriptures. I knew and believed that Jesus died for both our sins and our sicknesses.

"But he was *wounded for our transgressions,* he was *bruised for our iniquities: the chastisement of our peace* was *upon him; and with his stripes we are healed."* Isaiah 53:5

"Who his own self bare our sins in his own body on the tree, that we, being dead to sins, should live unto righteousness: by whose stripes ye were healed." 1 Peter 2:24

It was Jesus' willing offering of Himself on the Cross that bore my sins. But the very same tormented body of Jesus, in His scourging and crucifixion, purchased for me the blessing of divine healing — *"by His stripes we are healed."* (NKJV)

Not only has sin been overcome. Sickness has been overcome. The Cross of Jesus Christ has conquered both sin and sickness. Healing is mine because of what Jesus accomplished at the Cross. Jesus Christ the Saviour is just as surely Jesus Christ the Healer. I knew Christ was and is my healer.

[God] said, "If thou wilt diligently hearken to the voice of the LORD thy God, and wilt do that which is right in his sight, and wilt give ear to his commandments, and keep all his statutes, I will put none of these diseases upon thee, which I have brought upon the Egyptians: for I am the LORD that *healeth thee."* Exodus 15:26

God identified Himself to Israel in a variety of names and ways. Here He revealed Himself to His people as *"Jehovah-Rapha"* — *"the Lord who heals you."*

Healing is not just something that God does. No, more than that, healing is part of God's very nature — *"I AM the Lord who heals you."* God was, is, and will continue to be a

Healer but not any healer but The Healer. Remember always, Eileen, that you serve a healing God who has declared that His intent towards you is, *"not [to] bring on you any diseases ... [but to be] the Lord who heals you."* This I had to hold tight to and claim this promise. I could and would hold tight to the Word of God which said *I was* healed by Christ's stripes. I just had to claim my healing by faith.

Furthermore, God's spiritual healing power extends to *all* our diseases and infirmities.

> *"Bless the LORD, O my soul, and forget not all his benefits: Who forgiveth all thine iniquities; who healeth all thy diseases"*. Psalm 103:2-3

Again, another Scripture that I claimed. The greatest of the Lord's 'benefits' is that He forgives all my sins! But the Psalmist here charges us not to forget another of the Lord's benefits — that is, He *"heals all our diseases."* All my diseases! None are too hard for Him. God heals them all. No illnesses are excluded from this great 'benefit'. Whatever disease I, you or a loved one may have, it falls under God's promise to *"heal all thy diseases."*

It was the same God I was praying and crying to. I knew Jesus Christ who saved me could also heal me. Jesus healed a broad range of illnesses — in fact, He healed 'every disease and sickness.'

> *"Jesus went about all Galilee, teaching in their synagogues, preaching the gospel of the kingdom, and healing all manner of sickness and all manner of disease among the people. And his fame went throughout all Syria: and they brought unto him all sick people that were taken with divers diseases and torments, and those*

which were possessed with devils, and those which were lunatick, and those that had the palsy; and he healed them." Matthew 4:23-24

Christians serve a healing Saviour, Jesus Christ. His heart is for 'the people.' The Gospel records abound with illustrations of the healing miracles of Jesus among the masses, the men and women on the street. He preached and taught, yes. But He also healed every *disease* and sickness among the people.

"Every disease and sickness" — Christ's healing power is without limit. His healing touch is available to everyone and that included me. There is no illness beyond His ability to cure. He healed them all, and He was going to heal me. I had to believe, and I had to claim the healing for me. I would say to you as you read this, don't hesitate to bring any healing needs to Jesus, because in His ministry of healing, He demonstrated His ability and His willingness to heal *"every disease and sickness among the people."*

One day the Sister in charge of the ward decided to ask the community rehab team to come and assess me. I was told to not build up my hopes as they offered rehabilitation in the community to those people who were already able to be out of bed and had some mobility. I was not that length in recovery and who knew if I ever would be. More tears. God stores our tears in a bottle the scripture states but by this stage it seemed my tears could fill a lake.

Against all odds the rehab team decided to give me an opportunity. They took into consideration my young age and my determination not to go to a geriatric unit. Also, they commented on my positive mental attitude and said it would serve me well. I know it was God's intervention on my behalf, and my total trust was in my great God, so I just praised and thanked God for this window of opportunity. This was the first positive move for me but the first of many more. It was extremely difficult times for both me and the family. The dining room was converted and became my bedroom as I could not go up the stairs to our bedroom there. A team of carers was put in place to come in four times a day to look after me. This was not the only care package. I was truly blessed because I had another team of professionals who came in several times a week. This team included a physiotherapist who worked on my paralysed limbs; an occupational therapist who tried to keep me motivated and alert by doing various tasks with my hands. These ladies were a breath of fresh air coming in and I truly felt motivated to push and stretch myself in all the tasks asked of me.

The Scriptures tell us in the Book of Ecclesiastes 9:10 *"Whatsoever thy hand findeth to do, do* it *with thy might."* That is exactly what I strived to do. I would remind the Lord of His word and tell Him I was doing as best I could but that was in mine own strength; He could give me more, much more strength and I was depending on that to aim higher and higher. The Lord loves His children to remind Him of His Word and when we do, He will act according to our faith.

Jesus Christ said in Matthew 9:29, *"According to your faith be it unto you."* I was like the father of the young man who was demon possessed. The father had brought his son for healing to Christ's disciples, but they could not cast the demon out. The father brought his son to Jesus and we read in Mark 9:23 *"Jesus said unto him. If thou canst believe, all things* are *possible to him that believeth."* We read in the next verse that the father cried out and said with tears, *"Lord, I believe; help thou mine unbelief."* This is just what I kept doing: *"Lord I believe, help thou mine unbelief."* While ill, day and daily, this was the prayer of my heart. In fact, this is the prayer of my heart every day right to the present day.

The demon fought back right in the face of Jesus as satan never wants to give in, but he was no match for the Son of God there and then and it is the same today. Christ overcame death, hell, and the grave and is victorious. The demon was not departing without leaving his mark, but although it appeared to the crowd that the young man was dead, not so when Christ is present. Christ is life itself. We read in verse 27: *"But Jesus took him by the hand, and lifted him up; and he arose."* Note the action of Christ here:

1. Christ reached forth His hand and took him by the hand.
2. Christ lifted Him up from the dirt and gutter of the road.
3. Christ gave him power to stand up on solid ground.

This is an important sequence of events. This was what I was praying and trusting for daily.

It would be nice to say all went well from here but that was not the case. I suffered a few more minor strokes that necessitated me having to be hospitalised each time, but, yet again, on discharge it was back to the same regime. Progress was slow but I was trusting God for healing and I truly believed it would come. I kept claiming the promises in His Word and standing on them. It was very difficult for the family as I was completely dependent on them. I must also say it was hard for them to see their wife and mother in such a state physically and emotionally and this mother still in her forties. Just too young!

However, there was another problem; I was a fighter and wanted to be as independent as possible. The frustration was unreal and caused more trouble. Here was someone who was always on the move, telling people how to do things correctly and in set timescales and, now not going anywhere or doing anything, with all the time in the world to do this 'nothing' in. One thing I was taught, and I, in turn, taught others, was to look for something positive in the bad and turn it around into something good. It is a good trait to have. I was determined to give my utmost to all the physiotherapist asked me to do. I was putting into practice Ecclesiastes 9:10, "*Whatsoever thy hand findeth to do, do it with thy might;*" I did fight to achieve, and some would say I fought too much and that was what caused the setbacks. Whatever people may think I know I did the right thing with a positive attitude.

What is in Your Hand?

Arts and crafts were my hobbies for as long as I can remember and at this time my painting became my lifeline. My dear mother taught me to knit and sew before I even commenced primary school. I loved to knit and sew. Any free time I had as a child would find me with a needle or knitting needles in hand creating something for my doll. As I grew up my mother recognised the talents I had and so encouraged me to learn to do much more with my hands. I learned many other crafts such as crochet, painting, pergamano, beading, and embroidery. My mother bought me a large tablecloth and I had this embroidered before I was ten years of age. It is one item in my home I cherish to this day.

It is a good thing for a female to keep their hands busy creating. In Acts 9:36-42 we read the beautiful and miraculous account of Tabitha better known to us as Dorcas. The both names are the same but in two different languages, the first being in Syrian and the second being in the Greek. She was a lady who blessed the ministry with her great sewing of coats and garments. Little did I realise that through my talents which my mother helped me to develop I too would later bless God's ministry. I will cover the gift of talent in another chapter but suffice to say here that I firmly believe the statement; "If you don't use it you lose it!" The Bible gives us a clear understanding of this principle.

When I was able to progress from my wheelchair to a Zimmer frame and then on to using two walking sticks, the occupational therapist encouraged me to paint my walking sticks. This proved to be incentive enough for me to work hard and fast to be no longer relying on them for support. Many people who have heard me relate this part of my testimony always wonder why that should have been. The problem for me was - PRIDE — my painting was not to a good standard. People would say I am a perfectionist. I was taught by my parents if a job was worth doing it was worth doing right. The problem was I am right handed, and it was my right side that was so severely affected so with little to no power in my hand and not able to control the movement of a paintbrush too well the painting was poor by any standard. I was embarrassed with my efforts as I knew I had been able to achieve more cosmetically pleasing results.

Another problem for me was my loss of speech, and then my short-term memory was also affected. Many of the words I could not recall or form, so I had to be taught how to talk again. It took a long time, but I got there in the end. The frustration of wanting to say something but you just cannot get the word out is not easy to explain. I could point to the item, such as, the chair but could not say the word. It was a long time before I overcame this. My son, Derek, says they taught me too well to talk. (He does love me.) Believe me, those who know me will tell you I can really talk. Praise God I can witness and confess Jesus Christ to others. I thought I had lost this privilege for good.

Time was going by and I was slowly improving but not the miraculous and instant healing I was expecting. Not that I can say I never doubted but as fast as doubt came in, I kicked it out as a lie from satan. Christ Himself said this; John 8:44, *"for he (satan) is a liar, and the father of it."* I was still trusting God for my healing no matter what. God had given me a promise one day as I studied His Word and prayed. It is found in Jeremiah 30:17, *"For I will restore health unto thee, and I will heal thee of thy wounds, saith the LORD."* I felt God had these words jump right of the page at me, so I claimed them there and then and stood on the promise God gave me. I stood by quoting the Scripture continually before God and reminding myself that God cannot lie.

I thank God He did heal me, and I can sing with great assurance:

Shackled by a heavy burden,
'Neath a load of guilt and shame.
Then the hand of Jesus touched me,
And now I am no longer the same.

He touched me, Oh He touched me,
And oh the joy that floods my soul!
Something happened and now I know,
He touched me and made me whole.

Since I met this blessed Saviour,
Since He cleansed and made me whole,
I will never cease to praise Him,
I'll shout it while eternity rolls.

He touched me, Oh He touched me,
And oh the joy that floods my soul!
Something happened and now I know
He touched me and made me whole.

(Words by Bill Gaither)

Sometimes we think because we did not see the manifestation of the healing immediately when we ask for it, we deem it as a lesser miracle if we have to wait for it. But if we relate this to money, many times we pray for a financial need and if someone comes knocking on the door with the cash that is great. But if someone posts a cheque it is also as great. Same with healings, they can come immediately as we pray or be released immediately but a fight takes place for the manifestation of the supernatural.

> *"Then said he unto me, Fear not, Daniel: for from the first day that thou didst set thine heart to understand, and to chasten thyself before thy God, thy words were heard, and I am come for thy words. But the prince of the kingdom of Persia withstood me one and twenty days: but, lo, Michael, one of the chief princes, came to help me; and I remained there with the kings of Persia."*
> Daniel 10:12-13

What are these verses telling you and me? God had left Daniel in the land of exile in Babylon, for although the Jews had left Babylon to return to Jerusalem again after being held captive for many years Daniel was not to be in that number. They were to return to rebuild the Temple and the city walls. God had still a work for Daniel to do. There are all sorts of hostile powers hard at work, both openly and secretly. As is clear from these two verses, the hostile powers were both physical and spiritual, they were men and demons. In other words, behind the scenes we are to see spiritual warfare. Behind the scenes we are to see principalities and powers, angels and devils, good and evil doing battle with each other. The enemies of the Lord and His people were trying to stir up the Persian court and the king. God had revealed to Daniel that there was to be great warfare. Concerned, Daniel wondered whether the people of God would win or lose; anxiously he wondered what the future would bring for his people.

In the face of the hostile powers and their attacks, one of Daniel's jobs in Babylon was to intercede before the king. By His providence we see that God had arranged things that Daniel could plead the case of the Jews before the king. But that wasn't his only job, as these two verses makes clear. We see that it is also Daniel's job to intercede on behalf of the Jews before the King of kings in heaven. In other words, Daniel was also called by the Lord to be a man of prayer on behalf of the people of God. In any event, Daniel could do as much for the Lord's cause while remaining at his post in Persia as the men who stood on Jerusalem's walls with a sword in one hand and a trowel in the other. In fact, a man of prayer is worth as much as a thousand fighting heroes — if not more.

In an army every soldier has his place. An army can't get by with combat troops alone; it also needs people to look after food and supplies. Furthermore, officers are needed to plan and lead the attack. Also, an army needs people who stay at home, who support them and pray for God's protection and leading. Actually, this last category should be first. I wish to state clearly here to you reading this, do not think, especially if you are old or sick, that you can be of no use in the great struggle to establish God's Kingdom. If you and I cannot do anything else, every day we can at least plead the cause of God's people before the throne of grace.

We see, too, how Daniel's prayers succeeded in bringing angels from heaven to earth. These angels formed an invincible heavenly guard around the people of the Lord, with the result that the plans of the enemy failed. In these verses you and I hear an angel talking to Daniel. He says, "Do not be afraid, Daniel. Since the first day... your words were heard..." To view this in proper perspective we must remember that up to this point Daniel had mourned and fasted for three weeks. For 21 days Daniel had prayed without ceasing. For 21 days Daniel had interceded before the heavenly court on behalf of the people of God because of the "great war" (verse 1).

What the angel declared was that Daniel's words had been heard in heaven on the very first day already. It didn't take 21 days to get through. It was not like our present-day telephone lines that we ring to speak to a friend and find the line busy. Daniel was not stuck in voicemail like we sometimes are. Daniel had been heard from the first day. I can rest assured just as you can rest assured, that our prayers are heard just as quickly as Daniel's. God does not favour certain persons over others. Nor is it that God will eventually hear us if only we keep on praying long enough and loud enough. From the very first instant the prayer is offered God hears our prayers.

After those 21 days, an angel appeared to Daniel. I notice there is a direct connection between Daniel's prayer and the angel's appearance. The angel says, "*...thy words were heard, and I am come for thy words.*" Thus, it was Daniel's prayer that brought the angel down from heaven, just as an angel later appeared to release Peter from prison when the church in Jerusalem prayed for him (Acts 12). Imagine that: the power of prayer is so immense that it can even call angels from heaven to earth to help God's people.

Daniel prayed for help and an angel appeared. What an answer! Though they could not see him, the angel's presence created such panic among Daniel's companions that they fled and hid themselves. If the angel had this effect on Daniel's friends, just imagine how it would terrify Daniel's enemies. In addition to this unnamed angel, you and I are told that God had also sent Michael, "one of the chief princes" and the commander of the heavenly host, to join in the battle. Thus, heavenly powers rushed to the assistance of the Jews as God's answer to Daniel's prayer.

There is something mysterious about the story in front of us. The army of angels did come to the assistance of Daniel and his countrymen – but they seemed to take their time. Daniel waited for 21 days before the angel appeared before him. By that time the battle and war could have been lost! Two facts are clear to me; the prayer is heard the very first day, but Daniel did not know this until the 21st day. Daniel waited three weeks before finding out his prayer was answered.

At this point it becomes clear to me that God sometimes makes you and I wait for a while before we see an answer to our prayers. We may have to wait for 21 days, which really isn't all that long. We may even have to wait for 21 years. Sometimes we may never see an answer to our prayers with our own eyes. It may well be that the prayer is answered but the answer does not become fully apparent until after our death.

It is worth me noting here that if Daniel was not a believer, he might have concluded from this that there was no God in heaven and that prayer was a waste of time. However, the main thing is not seeing an answer but believing an answer says Jesus, "*blessed* are *they that have not seen, and* yet *have believed*" (John 20:29). It comes down to this: even if I have never seen an answer to prayer, and what Christian can ever say that, I am still to believe that God hears the prayers sent up to Him. I feel one of the reasons Daniel 10 is in the Bible is to teach you and me this lesson. This chapter proves that God right away hears and responds to our prayers even if you and I cannot hear or see the answer.

Furthermore, the angel told Daniel that he was commanded on the very first day to go to the earth. What took him so long? Why did it take him 21 days to give Daniel an answer? The reason, he explained to Daniel, is that, "*But the prince of the kingdom of Persia withstood me one and twenty days."* What does this mean? It means that for three weeks a mighty but invisible battle was fought between the angel of light and the prince of darkness. It means that for 3 weeks Daniel's prayer was being answered. Daniel had asked that the attacks of the evil one be halted so that the city and temple of God could be rebuilt. For three weeks angels were putting devils to flight. That was the reason for the delay.

Who is the prince of Persia that resisted Daniel's angel? Since God's angels are spirits, we know the prince of Persia, likewise, cannot be a man of flesh and blood. Rather, he is an evil spirit, a devil. The evil spirit is given the title of prince. This means that though fallen he has power and authority. Later we hear of another devil that is called "the prince of Grecia" (Greece) (10:20). If nothing else, satan is a superb organiser. Nothing is left to chance in the great war that he wages against Christ and the church. Everything is planned, right down to the smallest detail. He is the king of darkness and under his rule are princes and assistants. These underlings he puts in charge of individual countries in order to work their evil influence on leaders and people alike.

The devil assigned to Persia was given the task of turning the king and officials against the Jews. It was he who sowed seeds of suspicion against the loyalty of the Jews. Daniel, as it were, pulls back the curtain that separates you and I from the spirit world. He gives us a glimpse of the battle behind the scene, a struggle that goes on today, a struggle that goes on all around you and around me, even though we do not see it with our own eyes.

Before I leave, it is worth me asking you to note that satan's princes use different weapons and different approaches in their work of evil. The Prince of Persia used evil thought, jealousy, and hatred in order to stir up the leaders and people of Persia against the Jews. The prince of Grecia, whom I mentioned earlier, uses an entirely different approach. He tried to wipe out the people of God by getting them to conform to the ways of the world. His plan was to make the Jews breathe in Greek culture and Greek customs and Greek language so that they no longer were different or distinct from the peoples of the world.

Satan had tried to get the people to compromise just a tiny little way and once he got them to take the first step, he knew he had them hooked and to have them compromise more and more was much easier. Isn't that the way satan operates with you and me? He tempts you and me to make little compromises that seem so insignificant and ends up ensnaring us in sin. That is why I had to then and have to now, choose not to give a fraction when tempted.

It is the same for each country and each people; there are different demons with different weapons and different approaches. But they all have the same goal: to bring about the defeat and destruction of Christ and His church. The air above Israel, above the United Kingdom, Europe, Africa, and every country in the world is full of satanic forces and spirits. But, as sure as there are these evil forces the air is also filled with angels.

Remember verse 13 also states: "*but, lo, Michael, one of the chief princes, came to help me; and I remained there with the kings of Persia.*" So, in that anxious hour when Israel was under attack and in danger of quitting the job of rebuilding, the Lord's angels descended from heaven to do battle with the prince of Persia and the prince of Grecia. How tempted we are to run in despair when clouds of trials and temptations come our way. I'm sure Daniel was tempted to do that as he thought about the great war; but he did not! If we would look closely at our situation through the eyes of faith, we would see God's angels of mercy coming to our aid.

This reminds me of the story of Elisha and his servant (2 Kings 6). The king of Aram sent his soldiers to capture Elisha. During the night they surrounded the city of Dothan, where Elisha was staying. When Elisha's servant got up and saw the army with horses and chariots that surrounded the city, he was very alarmed. In 2 Kings 6:16, Elisha said, *"Fear not: for they that* be *with us* are *more than they that* be *with them."* And Elisha prayed a wonderful prayer in verse 17, *"and said, LORD, I pray thee, open his eyes, that he may see. And the LORD opened the eyes of the young man; and he saw: and, behold, the mountain* was *full of horses and chariots of fire round about Elisha."* You and I may not see the spiritual battle being waged around us. We may not see or feel the demons and angels, but they are there, and you and I should realize that. *"Fear not: for they that* be *with us* are *more than they that* be *with them"*.

I trust the place of prayer in the struggle between good and evil. When Daniel prayed the Lord sent down His angels to do battle. It is prayer that mobilizes the forces of heaven against the forces of hell. It is through prayer that the powers of wickedness, hatred, brutality, and injustice are broken.

Paul says the very same thing to the church at Ephesus. In our struggle he writes: *"we wrestle not against flesh and blood, but against principalities, against powers, against the rulers of the darkness of this world, against spiritual wickedness in high* places." These satanic forces and demons are very real today as they were away three thousand plus years ago. I hope, then, that you realise there is an enemy that surrounds you and I, an enemy unseen and unheard, an enemy who wants to strike us down. I hope also that you and I, like Daniel, pray for the Lord's angels to guard and protect and give us the victory so that Christ gets all the glory. I hope I never forget, and you never forget this great 'Fear Not'. "*Fear not: for they that* be *with us* are *more than they that* be *with them*". (2 Kings 6:16).

I believe satan knew what God had in store for me and he fought to not allow the healing. God, I also believe, allowed satan to have his way for a limited time and then God would turn it around for great blessing in my life. For me it was not instant healing, but God did heal me and the miracle as shared, was no less. Of course, I would have loved for God to heal me immediately but that was not the will of God. Why was it not His will I hear you ask? Let me tell you here. Although the devil had thought that I would go under with depression and even perhaps curse God for my illness God was going to turn it around for my good, the good of others and to the glory of God. I was stubborn and had gone my own way for many years and God had much to teach me. You see, God was teaching me many things during this period which I choose to call my "backside of the desert experience."

What did you learn I hear you ask? I learned what it was like for non-disabled people to block entrances, park in disabled car park spaces, close the shop door while Ian and I was struggling with me being in a wheelchair. Am I complaining here? No, because it reminded me of times when I looked out for myself, but when you know a disabled person could need that space, requiring to walk up the aisle, then I purposely prepare the way for that person coming after me. What I learnt most, is to seek to be like Jesus. For in all honesty, not one of us can walk the path of Christ, except through His grace. His grace is manifested through our life with Him going before us preparing the way, knowing Eileen Miller needs all the help I can to walk in His steps.

I remember the first time I was out in my wheelchair. Ian had taken me to Ballymena to the Tower Centre shopping centre to view the shops. We were only in a very short distance when we met people we knew. They looked at Ian and asked him, "How is she progressing?" I was so annoyed. It was like they were speaking in code as if I was not there. I may have lost the use of my legs and such, but I had not lost the use of my brain. It was a hurtful experience. I could feel my flesh rising, wanting to shout at them and tell them to speak to me directly, but they had left as quickly as they came. It was hard to accept and hard to cope with what was happening. I found myself not wanting to go out and if I did, I was on a very 'short fuse'.

This was a major issue with me and as a result I know, in turn, that when I meet people in similar circumstances, to always speak to the person being cared for before I speak with the carer. This is just one of many lessons God taught me. A further lesson I was to learn from this experience was the truth of the Scripture found in Romans 8:28 *"And we know that all things work together for good to them that love God, to them who are the called according to* his purpose." It did take time but a few years down the road of life I was to prove just how tremendous a truth there is in this great Scripture. If we trust God with all things knowing that He has the perfect plan for our life God can overturn anything and bring about the fulfilment of His purposes.

Later, when I was on my feet again though still not in the position to drive, I was asked to speak at a meeting. I did so not knowing that this was God opening a door to a new chapter in my life. I was invited to speak at many more meetings and soon it became the norm for me to be a regular speaker around the churches up and down our country.

When I asked God to heal me and vowed I would serve Him to the very best with all He gave me, I also promised that at every opportunity afforded me I would share the good news of saving faith in Jesus Christ. Another vow I made was that I would never finish a meeting without telling the congregation they needed to be saved and extending an invitation for people to come forward and give their life to Christ. You may say this is not necessary and I should just give a heartening and uplifting message, but the answer is a forthright "No!" While I was in my career, I answered to man, but now I am a servant of the King, I answer to God. God is my 'Boss' and I must abide by the job description given to me. Anyone who is given the opportunity of sharing the Word of God is called on to "Rightly divide the Word of God." When God opened this door to share the Word, He also gave me a Holy ambition which is found in 2 Timothy 2:15, *"Study to shew thyself approved unto God, a workman that needeth not to be ashamed, rightly dividing the word of truth."* This is the duty of all ministers, evangelists, pastors, and teachers. It is my duty, too, to please God by studying the Bible and then feed the 'flock' with the precious truth of Scripture. With God's grace I plan to do this, and we should never offer apologies for doing so.

No matter where I am speaking, I always tell the people their need of Salvation. Every person is born in sin and therefore sinners. Christ loves them and died on Calvary's cross, shed His precious Blood and bore the sins of the world on His body. Christ was buried but on the third day He rose again and ascended to the Father where He is seated on the right-hand side forever making intercession for us. There is power in the Blood to cleanse from all sin and there is power in the very name of Jesus. Hallelujah, what a Saviour! I love Him because He first loved me. But what does this really mean? Let me take a moment and explain God's plan of Salvation for you and for me.

God's Simple Plan of Salvation

I want to ask you the most important question of your life. Your joy or your sorrow for all eternity depends upon your answer. The question is: Are you saved? It is not a question of how good you are, nor if you are a church member, but **are you** saved? Are you sure you will go to Heaven when you die? Let me show you what God says in His Holy Word.

God says in order to go to Heaven, you must be born again. In John 3:7, Jesus said to Nicodemus, *"Ye must be born again."* In the Bible God gives us the plan of how to be born again which means *to be saved.* His plan is simple! You can be saved today. How? First, you must realize you are a sinner. *"For all have sinned,* and *come short of the glory of God"* (Romans 3:23). Because you are a sinner, you are condemned to death as I too was before I prayed in repentance. *"For the wages of sin is death"* (Romans 6:23). This includes eternal separation from God in Hell; *"it is appointed unto men once to die, but after this the judgment"* (Hebrews 9:27).

But God loved you and me so much He gave His only begotten Son, Jesus Christ, to bear my sins and your sin and die in your place; *"he hath made him (Jesus)* to be *sin for us, who knew no sin; that we might be made the righteousness of God in him"* (2 Corinthians 5:21). Jesus had to shed His Blood and die. *"For the life* of the flesh is *in the blood"* (Leviticus 17:11); *"without shedding of blood is no remission (pardon)"*

(Hebrews 9:22). *"God commendeth his love toward us, in that, while we were yet sinners, Christ died for us"* (Romans 5:8).

Although we cannot understand how, God said my sins and your sins were laid upon Jesus and He died in our place. He became our substitute. It is true. God cannot lie. *"God... commandeth all men everywhere to repent"* (Acts 17:30). This repentance is a change of mind that agrees with God that one is a sinner, and agrees with what Jesus did for us on the Cross.

In Acts 16:30-31, the Philippian jailer asked Paul and Silas: *"Sirs, what must I do to be saved? And they said, Believe on the Lord Jesus Christ, and thou shalt be saved."* Simply believe on Him as the one who bore your sin, died in your place, was buried, and whom God resurrected. His resurrection powerfully assures that the believer can claim everlasting life when Jesus is received as Saviour.

"But as many as received him, to them gave he power to become the sons of God, even to them that believe on His name" (John 1:12). *"For whosoever shall call upon the name of the Lord shall be saved."* (Romans 10:13). "*Whosoever*" includes you and includes me. "*Shall be saved*" means no questions asked, but "*shall be saved.*" That is your promise and my promise. Surely, you realize you are a sinner. Right now, as you read this, repent and lift your heart to God in prayer.

In Luke 18:13, the sinner prayed: *"God be merciful to me a sinner."* Pray: "Oh God, I know I am a sinner. I believe Jesus was my substitute when He died on the Cross. I believe His shed Blood, death, burial, and resurrection were for me. I now receive Him as my Saviour. I thank You for the forgiveness of my sins, the gift of Salvation and everlasting life, because of Your merciful grace. I pray in Jesus' name. Amen."

Just take God at His word and claim His Salvation by faith. Believe, and you will be saved. No church, no lodge, no club, no good works can save you. Remember, God does the saving. All of it! God's simple plan of Salvation is: You are a sinner. Therefore, unless you believe on Jesus Who died in your place, you will spend eternity in Hell. If you believe on Him as your crucified, buried, and risen Saviour, you receive forgiveness for all your sins and His gift of eternal Salvation by faith. "*For what shall it profit a man, if he shall gain the whole world, and lose his own soul?*" (Mark 8:36). Be sure you are saved. If you lose your soul, you miss Heaven and lose all. Please! Let God save you this very moment.

God's power will save you, keep you saved, and enable you to live a victorious Christian life. "*There hath no temptation taken you but such as is common to man: but God* is *faithful, who will not suffer you to be tempted above that ye are able; but will with the temptation also make a way to escape, that ye may be able to bear* it" (1 Corinthians 10:13).

Do not trust your feelings. They change. Stand on God's promises. They never change. After you are saved, there are three things to practice daily for spiritual growth:

- Pray — you talk to God.
- Read your Bible — God talks to you.
- Witness — you talk for God.

AFTER you are saved, you should be baptised in obedience to the Lord Jesus Christ as a public testimony of your Salvation, and then unite with a Bible-believing church without delay. "*Be not thou therefore ashamed of the testimony of our Lord...*" (2 Timothy 1:8).

Please note that you don't have to be baptised to go to Heaven. However, once I was saved, I knew that to be obedient to God I was to be baptised. In Acts 2:38 we read that Peter, when he was coming to the end of preaching said unto them; *"Repent, and be baptized every one of you in the name of Jesus Christ for the remission of sins."* It is a step of obedience for the believer. In verse 41: *"Then they that gladly received his word were baptized:"*

> Also, in Acts 8:12, *"But when they believed Philip preaching the things concerning the kingdom of God, and the name of Jesus Christ, they were baptized, both men and women."*

It is right and scriptural to follow through with baptism after we give our life to Christ. I was so privileged to be baptised in the River Jordan as Christ Himself was baptised there by John the Baptist.

> *"John did baptize in the wilderness, and preach the baptism of repentance for the remission of sins. And there went out unto him all the land of Judaea, and they of Jerusalem, and were all baptized of him in the river of Jordan, confessing their sins. And John was clothed with camel's hair, and with a girdle of a skin about his loins; and he did eat locusts and wild honey; And preached, saying, There cometh one mightier than I after me, the latchet of whose shoes I am not worthy to stoop down and unloose. I indeed have baptized you with water: but he shall baptize you with the Holy Ghost. And it came to pass in those days, that Jesus came from Nazareth of Galilee, and was baptized of John in Jordan. And straightway coming up out of the water, he saw the heavens opened, and the Spirit like a dove descending upon him: And there came a voice from heaven,* saying, *Thou art my beloved Son, in whom I am well pleased."*
> Mark 1:4-11

When we go under the water it is symbolic of dying to sin and as we rise out of the water we are rising to newness in Christ Jesus. It was a very memorable day for me as it is for anyone on their baptismal. It is also an outward sign of our confession of faith in Christ. *"Whosoever therefore shall confess (testify of) me before men, him will I confess also before my Father which is in heaven"* (Matthew 10:32). Go and tell others what Christ has done for you. Be not ashamed of your Saviour because He is not ashamed of you.

Delays are not Denials

God's delays are certainly not His denials. Time passed by and ten years later I was totally healed and out serving the Lord but looking back I can say God was with me every step of the way. I had plenty of time to read and study the Word of God; plenty of time to reflect but most of all plenty of time to wait for God. There was so much I was taught and so much good came out of this period of testing and of time that I was set aside by God. God had much to teach this wayward child and He brought me to a place where He could have my full attention. I thank God He loved me enough to chastise me.

Remember the children of Israel? God led them out of Egypt's slavery and bondage (Exodus 12) and was taking them into the promised land of Cannan which was a rich and fertile land. They moaned and complained continually. Moses, their leader must have got fed up with them. They wandered in the wilderness for 40 years. A journey that should have taken only eleven days took 40 years. Around and around the mountain they kept wandering wanting to submit to God's direction. They were distracted with the desires of the flesh and lost their direction. They wanted the good things of life at the cost of losing fellowship with God.

I was not much different. I wanted the good things in life at the cost of serving God so when the time came for me to recognise God, He had much teaching to do. God knows me better than I know myself and if I had been healed immediately, I possibly would have quickly forgotten where He had brought me from and returned to my career again. However, through my wilderness God taught me patience and God taught me how to study the Word and to claim the promises. He taught me how to praise and worship despite my feelings. Feelings are emotions that are ruled by the head, but a relationship is ruled by the heart. My heart had to be made right with God. It was a long learning process. I look back now and thank God He loved me so much that He allowed me this period of learning even though it was a time of trial and going through the fire.

I can now look back with perfect vision and say I am so glad He delayed. So glad He taught me so much. So glad that I experienced the closeness of God throughout those years and so glad to know that He was turning my nightmare experience into something wonderful that would glorify Him. People all over the world would learn of this great miracle God did in my life and people would turn to Christ through the witness. Friend you and I can still experience healing from God today. If you think God is not answering, hold on tight because the answer is on its way. For me the answer was delayed but not denied. It is the same for you as God has not changed. I do regret that I had not truly loved my Lord and Saviour, put Him first in my life, and then I could have served Him through all those wasted years.

Wasted years, wasted years Oh how foolish,
As I walked on in darkness and fear.
Turn around, turn around God is calling
He's calling me from a life of wasted years.

By Clyde Julian Foley (June 17, 1910 – September 19, 1968),
better known as Red Foley, was an American singer

But the Lord has promised to restore those wasted years to me and with His grace and mercy I will give Him my all to the day I die.

> *"I waited patiently for the LORD; and he inclined unto me, and heard my cry."* Psalm 40:1

I have proved this, dear friend reading this, and you may prove it too. Let us look at the first three verses of this Psalm very closely. It is David's testimony and "Praise God" it is my testimony also but more importantly it is God's Word to each of us. You and I need to eat this word and digest it. Why? Let us look and see what the entire Bible instructs us on this subject.

> *"All scripture is given by inspiration of God, and is profitable for doctrine, for reproof, for correction, for instruction in righteousness: That the man of God may be perfect, throughly furnished unto all good works."* 2 Timothy 3:16-17

The Greek says, "All Scripture is God breathed," which means it is the Word of God and therefore infallible. God gave the Word to his chosen servants and it is that spoken Word direct from God which is infallible. Everything you and I believe and teach must be founded purely on the word of God. It is also our map and compass for direction and travel. It also is the only guide for instruction and if we fully read, feast and study the Word properly that we understand it in turn it will produce a godly life in us.

When we come to look closer at waiting and what it means to wait patiently let us look first at Christ. It is worth noting that Jesus Christ was perfection itself in patience. Throughout His agony in the garden, His trial before Herod and Pilate in the Great Hall and throughout His passion on the Cross at Calvary patience was clearly manifested. This was a particular characteristic of Jesus Christ. He never murmured, He never complained, He never grew impatient, and He uttered not a word in anger. Christ waited patiently on His Father God Almighty. What an example for us to emulate, but do we? Christ our Saviour did what we need to do each day. He went to the 'secret' place. He had a secret place where He went to get alone with the Father. You and I, too, need a secret place. Where is your 'secret' place? Do you even have a 'secret' place? Only you can answer that before God.

There was a garden known as the Garden of Gethsemane. It was located across the Kidron valley from Jerusalem on the Mount of Olives. We are not told much about this garden other than it was a place Jesus went to pray.

> *"And Judas also, which betrayed him, knew the place: for Jesus ofttimes resorted thither with his disciples."* John 18:2

It was this garden that Jesus took His disciples and there He prayed the Father to take the cup of crucifixion and suffering from Him, but He was willing to do what His Father wanted. It is synonymous with Christ and His great agony. It was also where a mob, along with Judas Iscariot (who betrayed Christ with a kiss), came to find Christ. There they then arrested Him and led Him away to face trial by the Sanhedrin.

> *"Then cometh Jesus with them unto a place called Gethsemane, and saith unto the disciples, Sit ye here, while I go and pray yonder. And he took with him Peter and the two sons of Zebedee, and began to be sorrowful and very heavy. Then saith he unto them, My soul is exceeding sorrowful, even unto death: tarry ye here,*

and watch with me. And he went a little further, and fell on his face, and prayed, saying, O my Father, if it be possible, let this cup pass from me: nevertheless not as I will, but as thou wilt. *And he cometh unto the disciples, and findeth them asleep, and saith unto Peter, What, could ye not watch with me one hour? Watch and pray, that ye enter not into temptation: the spirit indeed* is willing, but the flesh is weak. *He went away again the second time, and prayed, saying, O my Father, if this cup may not pass away from me, except I drink it, thy will be done. And he came and found them asleep again: for their eyes were heavy. And he left them, and went away again, and prayed the third time, saying the same words. Then cometh he to his disciples, and saith unto them, Sleep on now, and take* your rest: behold, the hour is at hand, and the Son of man is betrayed into the hands of sinners. *Rise, let us be going: behold, he is at hand that doth betray me. And while he yet spake, lo, Judas, one of the twelve, came, and with him a great multitude with swords and staves, from the chief priests and elders of the people. Now he that betrayed him gave them a sign, saying, Whomsoever I shall kiss, that same is he: hold him fast. And forthwith he came to Jesus, and said, Hail, master; and kissed him. And Jesus said unto him, Friend, wherefore art thou come?* Then came they, and laid hands on Jesus, and took him." Matthew 26:36-49

Jesus went to the garden; He left the disciples and went a little further and fell on His face before God. He agonised in prayer. He cried unto God in agony and so intense was He in prayer before God the Father he sweat great drops of blood. God the Son had left the splendours of heaven knowing His destiny was the lonely hill of mount Calvary to lay down His life for me. If that isn't love, well, tell me what is then? He took on a mortal body for immortality to live and die so that you and I might be saved. In so doing He lived His life as the perfect sinless Son of God. One of the names for Christ is 'The Word'.

> *"And the Word was made flesh and dwelt among us."*
> John 1:14

No wonder we need to pray the Father to give us a mind and heart like Christ's. If Christ needed to wait upon God, and patiently, how much more do we? I pray, "Oh God may I reflect Christ in my life each day."

The Psalmist says he waited patiently and the Lord *"inclined unto me and heard my cry."* Psalm 40:1 We never ever wait on the Lord in vain. Please note this very carefully child of God; Neither Jesus Himself or any member of the body of Christ shall ever wait upon the Lord in vain. Bury this truth deep in your heart and feed upon it in days of trial, in days of tribulation, in days when you struggle and in days of waiting.

An Introduction to the Psalmist David

Let us take time to look at the Psalmist first before we continue with this study.

David was born to Jesse, and he was the youngest of eight sons. The date of his birth was 1085 BC; the place of birth was Bethlehem, and he was a descendant of the tribe of Judah. When God rejected Saul, He sent Samuel to anoint one of Jesse's sons to be king. After all the seven sons in the home were rejected, Samuel enquired if there were any more sons. Jesse remembered wee David away looking after the sheep. He was only a mere shepherd and a young boy, but God's ways are not our ways and He chooses the weak and the foolish things of this world to confound the wise. This shepherd boy was anointed by God to be King of Israel. David's training as a shepherd boy with a staff and a sling may seem to some to be very small, but David had to prove himself to God in the small things before God could entrust him with greater things.

David slew the lion and the bear rescuing the lamb, unharmed each time, right out of the fierce animal's mouth. Then David used the sling to kill the enemy of his people, the mighty giant Goliath and won the battle for the Israelites in the name of the Lord. David knew where his strength lay — not in anything of himself but in God alone. Then David was called to play music to help lift the depression from Saul. Yes, the depression lifted but Saul saw David as a threat and became so jealous that he sought ways to murder David. Jealousy is a dreadful demon. Saul was no different to the leaders of today. When in need call David! When the problem was solved, or averted, jealousy sprang up and opposition became the norm. Saul had promised David his daughter, Mareb, if he was able to kill Goliath and win the battle for his people, but when the Philistine was dead, and the Philistine armies put to flight, Saul soon forgot his promise and Merab was given to another. Later Saul asked for proof of one hundred dead Philistines by David and Saul would reward him with his daughter Michal. Now David was told that Michal loved David, so David bought proof to Saul of two-hundred dead Philistines. Saul had no option but allow David to have Michal as his wife. God's plans for David to have a wife who would love him and be a help meet were fulfilled.

The oldest daughter Merab would not have been the right one for David. God's choice is always the best. David was faithful to God until He committed adultery with Bathsheba and then arranged for her husband to be put in the front line of the battle to be killed. He thought he could cover up his sin, but you cannot hide from God. There are two things you cannot run away from. One is a mother's love and the other you cannot run from God. Sin has its consequences and sin has its price. God ordered Nathan to tell David his sins were exposed. However, the sin would not cost him wrathful and eternal punishment, but he would be fearfully chastised in his life. This son from David's adulterous relationship died in infancy. Several of his family would also come to an untimely end and some of his wives were raped in public. David had to pay the price of sin, but he repented, and God forgave him. This is the man God said was: *"A man after his own heart."*
1 Samuel 13:14

We read his prayer of confession and repentance in Psalm 51. David is regarded as the greatest King of Israel and is one of the most prominent figures in the history of the world. He is the most famous ancestor of Christ. Jesus is not called the "Son of Abraham" or the "Son of Jacob"; He is called the "Son of David."

David's life was filled with noble deeds, fine aspirations, and splendid achievements yet his life was stained with gross sin. No other character more fully illustrates the moral range of human nature.

You may wonder if it is necessary to take time to look at the life of David. I have done so, not really because of David as such, but rather that you and I can see and learn from it. It is imperative that you and I understand how David remained in favour with God. This was possible because David repented to God with a broken and contrite heart.

Our life is very similar to David's in many ways. You and I have sinned big time even though we say we are walking with God. The human nature or perhaps a better term is the carnal man reveals himself in our lives. We say with Paul, *"For the good that I would I do not: but the evil which I would not, that I do."* Romans 7:19

If I am totally honest before God each one of us knows this is true in our own life. Every day I let the Lord down in word or deed or in both but thank God His mercies are new every morning to you and to me. I do not have to save mercies from yesterday to carry over to this day but rather I know with assurance that there are new mercies given to me today and every day from the hand of God. Do you fully understand this? I want you to grasp this great truth and hold onto it with all your might and claim it for yourself. We can take heart from the account of David because, although we sin and fail God many times, when we confess and repent, He picks us up, dusts us down, and sets us on the right path again. His goodness is unlimited to us, but His mercies and grace are given though we do not deserve them.

With having looked at the background of David it will help us to move on and study these verses he wrote under inspiration of God. As I do this, I want to apply it to my own life and ultimately you, the reader, may apply it to your life also.

There are seven points and headings I want us to consider in David's testimony in Psalm 40 are:

1. God encouraged David — by listening (verse 1)
2. God lifted him up —by Salvation (verse 2a)
3. God set him up — by firm foundation, feet on solid rock (verse 2b)
4. God held him up — by Christ Jesus (verse 2b). The rock being Christ Jesus who holds us
5. God tuned him up — by putting a new song in his mouth (verse 3a)
6. God toned him up — by many shall see and fear (verse 3b)
7. God takes him up — upon death to heaven (Psalm 23:6) The Psalmist had already this assurance

Let us apply them to ourselves then.

1. God encourages us

I want you to notice there is no reference to sickness here. I do not believe David was sick outwardly, but I believe inwardly he was very sick. He was in the backside of the desert spiritually speaking and was going through conflict, dreadful conflict, and he knew exactly what he had to do. Not lift the telephone to phone a friend and complain. Not take to his bed and wallow in self-pity. Not wring the hands and cry, "Why me Lord? What have I ever done to deserve this?" He did not stop fellowshipping with other believers in church because they "do not know what I am going through, and they just do not understand." None of these! David knew he had to go directly to God. He had to go into the sacred place and fall before God crying out to Him alone. David also knew he had to wait there patiently until the Lord met with him and heard his cry. In waiting for God, he waited. The answer did not come quickly but David knew where his help would have to come from. It had to come from God above. He expected relief from no other but God alone and he never doubted but it would come in due season. There is power enough in God to help the un-worthiest of all people that trust in Him. David waited patiently but he continued believing, trusting, and praying until relief did come from God.

That was what I went through in my 'backside of the desert' experience. I have been honest with my testimony of this time of my life sharing all my own weakness and failures. When I could talk again, I did lift the telephone to a friend and bend their ear as I grumbled. I did ask "why me Lord?" There were days over those 10 years when I did get depressed and could have taken to my bed. Possibly the only reason I did not was because the carers were coming in each morning to get me up washed and dressed. I did not fellowship with others for a long period of time because I did not want to go to my church in a wheelchair. Again, pride was there. Further, I did not want people to talk to me and say to me the old much worn phrase 'I know how you feel.' That made me angry. Nobody could know how I was feeling unless they had been through a similar experience and few people in my church had. I did not need people to pull me down into the valley of depression more than I was. A truth I learned the hard way was, "If you want to soar like an eagle don't be surround by turkeys." If I wished to fight negative thoughts I had to come apart from negative people. Some people's speech was so depressing that if I was not depressed before I certainly was by the time they finished. Oh dear.... what was God trying to teach me? Patience!

Just like David I was learning from this that I needed to go to God and to wait with patience. I had to ask God to give me patience. I felt like the little child who prayed, "God give me patience but please hurry." However, I learned that I could do so with great assurance. Those who wait on the Lord can be confident they do not wait in vain. Eileen waiting on the Lord was not waiting in vain. For me it was as found in Isaiah 40:31, *"But they that wait upon the LORD shall renew* their *strength; they shall mount up with wings as eagles; they shall run, and not be weary;* and *they shall walk, and not faint."*

Remember, dear brother and sister, God's timing is always perfect. He knows exactly when to answer, how to answer, and in what manner to answer our cries. Jesus cares. Jesus cared for David, He cares for you, and He cares for me. Get into the secret place and cry out to God alone. Child of God, wait patiently for Him and your strength will be renewed. Jesus is the only one who needs to know. We should always go to God first. But it is hard to go to God if you have not been talking to Him. Talk to Him daily as He is your best friend. I had to learn this lesson. I confess I was a slow learner but better slow than not at all.

Keep Short Accounts with God

My mother often used to say to us, "Keep short accounts with God." This can only be done if you and I are in constant communication with Him through prayer. I need to have intimacy with God. You need to have intimacy with God. I want to ask you a question that I had to ask myself also. If an emergency was to arise in the home and family who would you and I go to first; our husband or parents — maybe for you reading this, it would be your wife or close friend? Why would I go to my husband? Because of the close bond we both have, and my spouse knows me better than anyone else. I trust he will understand where I am coming from. He will understand my reaction and understand my feelings and concerns. For us females, and me especially, the husband will take over control and sort everything out giving me peace of mind again. Friend, that is what Jesus Christ should be like to you and me. I should know to go to Christ first. The next step then after going to Christ is to consciously and determinately hand all over into His hand. If I do take this second step of faith, then my third step follows which is by faith to wait on the Lord and He will renew my strength. He will give me peace as He answers my prayer of faith. The outcome is that I shall then mount up on wings like eagles and I shall run and not faint. Isaiah 40:31 He is Shalom — Hebrew for the "Prince of Peace" Isaiah 9:6. He is peace to my troubled soul. (Psalm 32:7-8; 81:7)

> *"When thou passest through the waters, I will be with thee; and through the rivers, they shall not overflow thee;"* Isaiah 43:2

Take encouragement today as David and Isaiah did, and as I do, that the Lord will always hear your prayer. You too can have that assurance that I had and still have today.

David paints a picture here of being in complete misery before the Lord lifted him up out. It is worth noting that David was despised by his brethren. In 1 Samuel 17:14, he was attending the sheep when his father asked him to take food to his brothers, who were fighting in the battle against the Philistines, and see how they were and bring a report back home.

> We read in verses 25-29, "*And the men of Israel said, Have ye seen this man that is come up? surely to defy Israel is he come up: and it shall be,* that *the man who killeth him, the king will enrich him with great riches, and will give him his daughter, and make his father's house free in Israel. And David spake to the men that stood by him, saying, What shall be done to the man that killeth this Philistine, and taketh away the reproach from Israel? for who* is *this uncircumcised Philistine, that he should defy the armies of the living God? And the people answered him after this manner, saying, So shall it be done to the man that killeth him. And Eliab his eldest brother heard when he spake unto the men; and Eliab's anger was kindled against David, and he said, Why camest thou down hither? and with whom hast thou left those few sheep in the wilderness? I know thy pride, and the naughtiness of thine heart; for thou art come down that thou mightest see the battle. And David said, What have I now done?* Is there *not a cause?*"

This was his brother who goes on to slay their enemy, the giant Goliath. If it had not been for David, the brothers and all the Israelites would have been in a very sorry state. They were all so scared of their enemies despite having the best military hardware of the day. David went in the strength of the Lord. (verses 45-47) This was the young boy who was chosen by God but scorned by his older brothers.

Remember Joseph? (Genesis 37:1) He was favoured of the father, but his brothers hated him. They were very jealous and cast him into a pit to leave him there to die. However, there was one of the brothers who took pity on Joseph and as a result Joseph was sold into slavery. Joseph was a type of Christ. A foreshadow of Jesus Christ. Christ was the beloved Son of the Father God. He was hated by the religious and political people of the day then and still is despised and rejected by men and woman today. Christ came to earth and died and shed His Blood on the cross of Calvary, bore your sins and mine on His body on the tree. He who did no wrong became sin for me and sin for you. He went down to the pit of hell and holds the keys of hell. He was victorious over death, hell, and the grave. (Hebrews 2:14; Revelation 1:18)

The problem for me was I owed a debt I could not pay but Christ paid a debt He did not owe. Through Him I have the victory and you reading this today can have the same victory. What encouragement this is for me to keep pressing on. The battle is not mine. The battle is the Lord's. (1Samuel 17:47; 2 Chronicles 20:15) Just like David said when facing Goliath that he came in the strength and name of the Lord when I face a Goliath in life, I too can say to it, *"I come to thee in the name of the LORD."* (1 Samuel 17:45) There is no greater name than I could ever put my trust in than the Lord's name.

2. God lifts us up

Christ is that sure foundation of my Christian faith and my faith is in Christ the Saviour of the world. I was in the pit of sin and darkness but when I cried out in repentance Christ drew me up with cords of love washed my sins away and saved me for all eternity. When we find ourselves in a pit full of mud and stinking dirt, we cannot help ourselves no matter how much we try. In fact, it is doubly sore and soul destroying because there is nothing firm to hold unto.

There is nothing solid to give the feet a firm grip to climb up out. I soon found out the more I tried by myself and in my own strength, to climb up out, my burden became heavier, and I grew weaker. I struggled and fought but to no avail. I had to confess that it was hopeless. Let me explain it this way, we expend all our energy and strength trying to achieve something that is hopeless and impossible within ourselves.

Same in the spiritual, we cannot help ourselves. Church membership, baptism either infant or adult, confirmation, clean living, doing good deeds, not smoking, not drinking, gambling or doing drugs, commendable though some of these are, will not get you and me into heaven. That is like trying to walk the clean side of the broad road, the dirty side being left for all those who are much worse and deeper in sin or gross sin. God does not categorise sin. We cannot read of this anywhere in scripture. His Word clearly states that sin is sin (Romans 3:9,23). If I was to attend a church where the preacher does not tell it as it is, it is incumbent of me to get out of there and go somewhere that the preacher preaches the truth and nothing but the truth according to the Word of God.

We need help to get out of the pit. There is a greater power required and that power I found in the person of Jesus Christ. Doctors, nurses, counsellors and preachers are all good in their own place but ultimately the only help worth counting on comes from the Lord. The psalmist says, *"I will lift up mine eyes unto the hills, from whence cometh my help. My help* cometh *from the LORD, which made heaven and earth."* Psalm 121:1-2

God was my helper back then and He is still my helper today. Only He can lift me up and out of the pit. What pit do you find yourself in today? Is it the pit of sin? I counsel you to come to Jesus. Come to the Saviour and make no delay for He is waiting to save you. Is it the pit of sickness or disease? The God who made us says in His Word we are *"fearfully* and *wonderfully made"* (Psalm 139:14) and He can heal you. I proved that all it takes is one touch of the Master's hand. Is it the pit of depression or despair and you feel you just cannot carry on? Life is just not worth living; well He will give a peace and turn your life around if you just allow Him. Elvis Presley recorded a hymn which I used to sing and today I can truly say Jesus is my reason for living:

I remember my days of darkness
Without sunshine or sight to lead the way
But a whisper of His voice softly calling
To the arms of my Maker to stay

He is my reason for living,
Oh He is the king of all kings
I long to be His possession,
Oh, He is my everything

Songwriters: DALLAS FRAZIER
He Is My Everything lyrics © Sony/ATV Music Publishing LLC

Are you in the pit of turmoil and stress? Christ can be your Shalom, which means He can give you peace, a peace that the world cannot give you. Are you being asked to go through a dark valley? Very often blessings only follow trials so I can expect to go through trials in my life. The Lord says He will go with me and you can claim that promise also. He will lead the way and if I cannot see He is the light unto my feet and a lamp unto my path. I claim these promises daily. These are facts about my great God, and these are promises for you and for me to hold unto. He will lift me up if I cry unto Him. He will lift you too if you cry unto Him. I urge you to taste and see that the Lord is good.

3. God sets us up

Not only did God lift me up and continues to lift me up out of the pit, as David says, but He gives me a sure foundation on which to place my feet to stand firm. When the storm came and more storms no doubt will come as I journey the road of life, my foundation is secure in Christ and therefore I can face the storm. I can say from my own personal experience in the words of the hymn writer:

I know the Master of the winds.
I know the Maker of the sea.
He can calm the storm and make the sun to shine again.
I know the Master of the wind

Sometimes I soar like an eagle through the sky
Above the peaks my soul can be found.
An unexpected storm may drive me from the heights
It may bring me low, but never brings me down.

I know the Master of the winds.
I know the Maker of the sea.
Let Jesus calm your storm, make the sun shine again
He is the Master of the wind.

(Gaither's Master of the wind)

I can say it with all surety but can you? Sometimes it is a severe storm that I have been in. The ship I am in that sails the sea of life gets a real tossing but with Christ in the ship with me I can say:

I have journeyed through the long, dark night
Out on the open sea, by faith alone
Sight unknown, and yet His eyes were watching me

Chorus:
The anchor holds
Though the ship is battered
The anchor holds
Though the sails are torn
I have fallen on my knees as I faced the raging seas
The anchor holds in spite of the storm

I've had visions, I've had dreams
I've even held them in my hand
But I never knew they would slip right through
Like they were only grains of sand

I have been young but I am older now
And there has been beauty that these eyes have seen
But it was in the night, through the storms of my life
Oh, that's where God proved His love to me

My anchor holds
Though the ship is battered.
My anchor holds
Though the sails are torn.
When I get down on my knees He calms the raging sea.
My anchor holds In spite of the storm.

(1994 Word Musicascap (a div. Of Word, Inc.) and Shepherd Boy Musicascap (adm. By Word, Inc.).
The Anchor Holds lyrics © Warner/Chappell Music, Inc.
Words and music by Lawrence Chewning and Ray Boltz)

When I am lifted up and my feet are on the solid rock I am as much elevated with the hopes of heaven as I was before I was saved and cast down with the fears of hell. Hallelujah! What a mighty God I serve. Angels bow before Him and heaven and earth adore Him. What a mighty God I serve. Of a truth He is my anchor and He is my sure foundation. What is more; when I praise Him, I get raised by Him. That is why I love my gospel music.

4. God holds us up

Many people say they do not want to give their life to the Lord because they could not keep it. That is true to a point, I cannot keep it, but Christ my Lord does all the keeping. As I walk along the rough road of life there are many potholes of temptation to fall into. Christ understands me being tempted because He, too, was tempted by satan but God says in His Word to, *"resist the devil and he will flee from you."* (James 4:7)

How did Christ resist the devil? He answered every temptation by quoting scripture to him. (Matthew 4:1-10) satan does not like the Word of God because He knows there is power in the Word. If I 'eat' the Word of God daily I will grow stronger and stronger as the days go by. Should I miss my meals for a day in the natural I will grow weak and it is the same in the spiritual. If I miss reading and meditating on the Word, I will start to grow weak in my faith. This is a question I put to all who profess Christ as Saviour. Are you feasting on the Word of God child of God? Are you on solid food or have you not grown up yet and still living on a little milk each day?

A little girl was always talking about Jesus to her classmates in primary school. The teacher thought she would put an end to the little girl's joy in the Lord, so she asked her in front of the whole class, "Tell me Ruth what do you do when the devil comes along to tempt you?" Ruth, in an instant, replied, "When the devil comes knocking on my door, I just ask Jesus to go and answer it." You and I might smile at the simplistic faith of the child, but the Word of God says we are to have faith like a little child. What does this mean? A child accepts what it is told by a grown up and no questions asked.

When I taught my children to pray, they were obedient. They would pray and take problems to the Lord that even I doubted on. I was given a profound lesson. We had kittens and they were as wild as could be. They were closed in an outside house and the children's job was to feed them and spend time working to tame them. It was winter time and only a couple of days had passed since we had got them. Derek was approximately seven years of age and this particular morning he went to take them their food. Minutes later he returned crying his eyes out. The kittens had bolted when he opened the door and were gone. I went back with him to see for myself and there they were on the very top of the ridge of the house. How they managed to get up so high is any ones guess but they were wild.

We came back in and he was not to be consoled. He then exclaimed, "I know, Mummy, what we will do. We will pray and ask God to bring the kittens back into the house again." Well, you can imagine my thoughts. Was God really concerned with such a trivial matter and anyway the kitten had made the great escape so would they want to return? I did not think so. Derek was sure God would answer because it was so cold and frosty the kittens would die if left out overnight. I took him to school and came back and prayed asking the Lord to please hear and answer my son's prayer for no other reason than to not have His faith in God shattered.

All day long I never caught a glimpse of the kittens and when time came to collect him from school, I dreaded answering the question I knew was going to be asked. Sure enough he asked had the kittens returned and I told him they had not. "Never mind, Mummy," he said. "There is still plenty of time until night and God will bring them back in safely."

Oh dear! The pressure was on and I silently prayed and asked God to please intervene for the sake of my child. Just before evening tea, Derek and I drove down the road again to collect his big sister coming on the bus from school. It was completely dark by now and as we were driving back into the yard the car lights shone on the outhouse straight ahead. We all saw it at the same time. The car lights reflected off the eyes of the kittens which were curled up together in the house.

Derek shouted, "There they are, Mummy. I knew God would bring them back in before bedtime." He jumped out of the car and ran over and shut the door on them. All I could do was bow my head over the steering wheel and weep because of my unbelief and give thanks to God for being so faithful in the small things but which were so major in my child's life. That night Derek thanked God for answering his prayer and looking after his kittens; I thanked God for the lesson I learned and asked forgiveness for my unbelief.

God says in His Word He holds us in the palm of His hand. That can read "Jesus holds Eileen in the palm of His hand. He bears me up least I dash my feet upon a rock." Now let's make this personal… let's put your name in the sentence as you read… "He holds _______ in the palm of His hand. He bears _________ up least I dash my feet upon a rock." (Matthew 4:6)

With this assurance from God it gives you and me another great promise to hold unto and speak out, *"I can do all things through Christ which strengtheneth me."* (Philippians 4:13)

Faith that Moves Mountains

Mountains have to move when people pray in the mighty name of Jesus Christ. God seldom takes us out of the valley, but He will lead us through the valley and as I put my hand in His. He holds me up in my faith. More; I can say He holds me up at all times. I have nothing to fear.

So, what is this faith that moves mountains? Well, it's the faith that we are to live by. We read in Hebrews 10:38, *'the just shall live by faith'*, and it is a quotation of the Old Testament book of Habakkuk 2:4. Yet is much, much more.

Prayer is a wonderful privilege. God has opened the door to His throne room and invited His children to enter His presence with their petitions, Hebrews 4:16. He has promised to hear us when we call, Jeremiah 33:3. And, he has promised to answer our prayers when we pray according to His will, 1 John 5:14-15. We all know that there are many privileges and promises associated with prayer. I want to remind us from this passage that prayer is also a very powerful endeavour.

Acts 12:5 reads, *"Peter therefore was kept in prison: but prayer was made without ceasing of the church unto God for him"*. It was fervent prayer. We are told that "*prayer was made without ceasing...*" The word '*ceasing*' means 'to stretch forth'. It is a medical term that refers to a stretched ligament or a pulled muscle. It has the idea of 'going beyond the boundaries'.

When applied to prayer, it is a picture of fervency. It is the picture of people pouring out their hearts in prayer before the Lord as they seek His face for their needs.

That's the kind of praying you and I need to undertake. The promise of God is that, *"the effectual fervent prayer of a righteous man availeth much,"* (James 5:16). The words *'effectual fervent'* refer to *'energetic passionate'* prayer. It is not prayer that is sluggish, lifeless, unconcerned, casual, half-hearted, blasé, and apathetic. It is prayer that pours forth from a burdened heart. A prayer that is prayed from the depths of the inner man, the very belly where the fire of God is raging is what I am talking about. That is the kind of prayer which reaches heaven and moves the hand of God.

It is good for you and me to note another important point about this prayer. It was faithful prayer. By faithful praying, I mean theirs was a prayer of faith. Their prayers were made *'to God'*. This seems obvious, but there are times when it seems like our prayers are designed to be heard by other people, or even by us. This congregation joined their voices and reached up as one to touch God for their church and for Peter. When you and I pray, we must pray in faith. Faith is the essential ingredient that marks the difference between answered and unanswered prayer.

The Bible makes these statements about the importance and place of faith in prayer:

> "*But without faith* it is *impossible to please* him: *for he that cometh to God must believe that he is, and* that *he is a rewarder of them that diligently seek him*."
> Hebrews 11:6

> "*And all things, whatsoever ye shall ask in prayer, believing, ye shall receive.*" Matthew 21:22

> *"And this is the confidence that we have in him, that, if we ask any thing according to his will, he heareth us: And if we know that he hear us, whatsoever we ask, we know that we have the petitions that we desired of him."* 1 John 5:14-15

Do I pray believing God can and will? Do you pray believing or do you still doubt? The last answer to prayer the circumstances were different.

I remind you, that when we pray, we are talking to our Father. He delights in hearing and answering the prayers of His children (Luke 12:32). I believe it is appropriate to say here that we need to always come to the Lord with respect and reverence. With this in mind I believe strongly that it is irreverent and wrong to address God, as 'Daddy'. It seems to be a new trend in some churches but if I have a clear knowledge of who God is, I will address Him as Father in accordance with the Lord's prayer.

It was focused prayer — Prayer was "*made... for him*". In other words, Peter was the focus of this prayer meeting. They came together to pray for a specific purpose. This was not generalized praying, that sought to cast a big blanket of prayer over everything and everyone. This was pointed prayer that sought God's power for a specific need. If you and I do not pray specific prayers, how will we ever know when God answers? When you and I ask Him for specific needs, and God answers, it glorifies Him, it assures us of our relationship to Him, and it increases our faith. All I am suggesting is that you and I need to be specific in our praying!

The last thing to note about this time of prayer in Acts 12 is: It was family prayer. They, as a church, gathered together to pray for one of their own. They came together as a family to seek God's help for a brother in great need. The church touched Heaven for Peter. Their prayers had power because they were united in their walk with God. They joined their hearts and their hands, then they lifted their voices to God, and He heard them and moved in power.

You and I may pray a lot, but I fear that we fail to pray for one another. Like me, you may be guilty of praying for my needs and my burdens, but how much time do you and I really spend praying for others? Right now, there are people in your church family and mine, who are facing life-threatening illness. You and I should be touching Heaven for them. There are others who are wayward. You and I should be touching Heaven for them. There are others who are struggling with needs, burdens, and problems. You and I should be touching Heaven for them. If you and I will take just a minute to think, the names and faces of our brothers and sisters in Christ will come to our mind. They need you and me to touch Heaven for them!

Your differences and mine hinder our prayers! We want to see people saved. We want to see the Lord bless the church. We want the power of God on us once more. You and I pray, and we pray, and we pray, but we do not see power of God manifested in our midst, and it is because we have allowed petty differences to divide us. I want to go on record and say that if I have offended you, I am sorry, but this needed to be said. I love you and I want to be able to join my voice with yours, so that we can touch Heaven together for the glory of God. This is the kind of prayer that moves mountains. It moved a mountain for Peter.

It was the night before Peter was to appear before Herod Agrippa. Peter was sleeping between two soldiers bound with two chains. There were two guards who looked after the security of the whole prison. An angel appeared unto Peter and a light shone all around him. The angel smote Peter on the side and raised him up quickly. The chains fell off his hands. The angel told him to get gathered up, put on his sandals and his garments and to follow the angel. Peter did as he was commanded by the angel but did not realise at first it was reality; he thought he saw a vision.

When they got past the first and second guards, they came to the iron gate that led unto the city. It opened before them and the angel and Peter went along the street where the angel then left him. "...when *Peter was come to himself , he said, Now I know of a surety, that the Lord hath sent his angel, and hath delivered me out of the hand of Herod, and* from *all the expectation of the people of the Jews.*" (Acts 12:11). Peter then proceeded to the house of John Mark's mother, Mary, where many of the church where meeting in prayer for Peter and his release. At first, they did not believe Rhoda when she said Peter was at the door. She recognised his voice without even opening the door and ran to tell them leaving poor Peter still outside the closed door. The people told poor young Rhoda she was mad but when Peter kept knocking and they came and opened the door we read that "they were astonished." How sad to be focused in their praying; praying so fervently and with faith but when the answer came, they doubted and were in total disbelief. I can identify with them because I have been guilty of the exact same reaction.

Let me share with you my own experience of focused, fervent prayer being answered. My husband and I were in Bible College and things were very tight financially. I went to Ian at lunch break on one Friday to share with him that I had no money for food. We had teenage children still at school and I knew they needed to be fed but what could I tell them when I would go home? We spent time in fervent prayer during our lunch break and when we came home, we continued crying unto God to provide for our immediate daily needs. It was real focused praying. I knew that God had fed the Children of Israel when in the wilderness (Exodus 16) but we were different. Did I have enough faith to believe God would do it for us? Oh, how I hoped so but... There is always a 'but' isn't there?

The children came in from school and I made a drink of tea for them, but Ian continued in prayer in the bedroom. My daughter asked me what would be for tea later and I just replied that I had not decided yet but there would be something. About an hour before tea I heard the letterbox drop so I went through to the hall. As I looked through the glass doors into the porch, I saw an envelope lying. I opened the outside door to see who was there, but nobody was standing. Furthermore, as I stepped out and looked up and down the footpath there was no one to be seen. After returning inside and closing the door I opened the envelope and to my surprise and shock, in it I found enough money to go to the supermarket and do a shop for tea.

I ran up to Ian and showed him what the Lord had done. We cried with sheer joy and gave thanks and praise to Almighty God. What a miracle and delivered right to our door by an unseen hand. Our God still hears and answers prayer. He is still the God of miracles. But that was not the end of this great miracle. A short time later our doorbell rang. Ian went to the door and on the doorstep, he found sitting a large box of groceries containing everything a family would need. Again, when Ian went to see who the person or persons who had left it and to thank them, he found no one. He looked up and down the street but there was absolutely no one around. The children were so amazed when Ian brought in the heavy box and there were a variety of things we had to make for tea. We jumped for joy and just kept praising the Lord. Then we gathered together and gave prayerful thanks to God for the amazing answer to our prayers. However, this still was not the end for that day. While I was preparing tea, the doorbell went again and when Ian answered there stood my sister and wee brother. She said she had decided to bake that day and had brought us down boxes of wee buns, shortbread, cakes, and tray bakes. It was like a feast and we were able to share with some of our other friends in Bible College. What a blessing it was to us and in turn we were able to share our blessing with others too.

5. God tunes us up

The psalmist was given a reason to rejoice and a heart to rejoice. There is an expression I heard first when I was at a large church in London. The senior pastor is called Pastor Denis Greenidge, a mighty man of God. I was there for their conference at Easter and experienced a mighty outpouring of the Holy Spirit in that church. There were many things I learned and was greatly blessed of God, but one thing was instilled upon my mind which I have shared with many since then. When preaching, Pastor Denis said, "If you complain you remain; but if you praise you will get raised." This is a very profound statement. Complainers and moaners are never happy unless they have something to complain about. You hear them say such things like, "it is so cold and wet today. My pains are playing up and I just wish the rain would go away and it would get nice and warm." When you meet again on a nice dry and sunny day, you expect them to be in better form but all you get is, "I can't stick this heat. It's far too warm and makes me so tired. I wish we had rain to water the flowers. We need rain badly." Can you imagine God listening to all this? I learned that if I kept company with those who moaned and complained I, too, would get just like them. I had to distance myself and, in all things, to give thanks to God and offer up my worship and praise to Him.

I love music and I love singing. That is one great characteristic of the people in Africa. They know how to worship and praise God. They dance and sing unto God just like David did in the temple. If there has been anointed praise and worship offered up, I find it makes it much easier to stand behind a pulpit and preach the Word. Good sincere praise and worship offered up as a sweet sacrifice to God means there is freedom for the Spirit to work. The church in London has tremendous praise led by the choir "Sincere Praise" aptly named, as the men and ladies are all born again as is their trainer and leader, Sister Jenny.

When I am cast down, I say to my soul, *"why art thou cast down, O my soul?"* (Psalm 42:5) David also says, *"Let the words of my mouth, and the meditations of my heart, be acceptable in thy sight, O LORD,"* (Psalm 19:14). I had to learn this lesson, too. I had to start and offer up praise and thanksgiving to the Lord and then I would soon be raised again. Another thing I have to do is to put on good anointed gospel music. I listen to the beautiful words and let the singing wash over and minister to my soul, even at times I would praise worship and sing along. A Pastor friend from Kisumu in Kenya, Pastor Tobias, was preaching and he said if we each were to sing in the mornings, we would find ourselves in a good spiritual place to go out and face the day. I have proved this and can guarantee that anyone who puts this into practice will also experience what I did; soon you will be in the Spirit lifting the name of Jesus and worshipping the Lord. The problems will have greatly decreased if not gone completely.

I remember in the olden days when very young I listened to all the worldly music and I knew all the words to sing along.

When I put my trust in the Lord, He changed even my very language. God took away the desire for worldly things and He put a new song in my mouth. I just want to keep singing the praises of God. I just want to keep rejoicing in the Lord. God has tuned me up to praise and worship Him. I do so with all that is in me. There is joy in my heart that is unspeakable and my heart is full of glory to my Lord and Saviour. How could I not sing praises to my God and King after what He has done for me?

Our Confidence is in God

6. God tones us up

When I have confidence in God I can boldly go where others fear to go but only where and when the Lord leads and guides me.

When I was in Kenya travelling with Pastor Godfrey Mugolo, who was my interpreter and minder, we spent a week in a particular village. There was a definite spirit of darkness all over, so great was it one could almost taste it. Continually we prayed claiming the covering of the Blood of Jesus Christ. We knew God had called us to go and take the gospel there. On the first Sunday morning after I had finished bringing the Word, I invited people to come forward and give their life to Christ. There were fifty-nine people responded to the invitation and we had the great privilege of leading them to the Lord and to pray the sinner's prayer.

Each day proved to hold its own difficulties for Pastor Godfrey and myself, but we prayed for the covering of the precious Blood over us and trusted the Lord. The people kept coming and even though there were thunderstorms some of the days, we managed to get through all the mud to reach the church. Sometimes during the crusade, the heavens would open, the rains would come down relentlessly, and we would get drenched, but Pastor Godfrey and I kept ministering even to the extent of preaching through the heavy rains. The people were not deterred, and souls were saved.

The next week we had moved on to another area and we were taken aback when one of the pastors, whom we knew well, asked us what had taken us to the other village the previous week. We asked what we thought was the obvious question; "why should we not go? The Lord had laid it heavily on our hearts to go and through much oppositions, the Lord had saved many souls and blessed us." We were then told that no white person went there as it was too dangerous. The area was under control of witches – many witches and the people were living under charms and curses. We proclaimed to the people that we were safe and felt safe because our confidence was totally in God and not in man. God had sent us, and we were just being obedient. God had protected us and given us much fruit for our labour.

In Christ we can do all things and in God I had put my trust as had Pastor Godfrey. The people had seen Christ in us and saw we trusted God. They wanted something. They were seeking something to fill the void in their life and they wanted what we had. There was a great hunger for the Word and the people were ripe for God's harvest. It was due time that someone went in and reaped the harvest of the Lord. This is exactly what God had called me to go and do and I was only being obedient to my calling.

These people had witnessed the witches taking all their money and goods for cures and charms but instead of people improving they were growing worse and dying and poverty was increasing.

A Healing Ministry

The Scriptures teach in James 5:14, *"Is any sick among you? let him call for the elders of the church; and let them pray over him, anointing him with oil in the name of the Lord:"*

The Bible does make it clear through several examples that the laying on of hands should be done when anointing the sick. The use of oil is not always mentioned, but when I look at the entirety of the passages and the admonition in James, I see that the oil is a vital part of the anointing. Remember, the word *anoint* means 'to rub with oil.' Mark tells the reader they *"anointed with oil many who were sick, and healed* them" (Mark 6:13). Oil represents God's Holy Spirit. I know it's not the oil that heals.

I also know it is not the elder performing the anointing who heals. Does it make a difference which elder does the anointing? After writing about being anointed by an elder, James tells me, *"And the prayer of faith shall save the sick, and the Lord will raise him up; and if he have committed sins, they shall be forgiven him."* (James 5:15) The oil I use is scented oil which I have chosen to set apart dedicated to the Lord's ministry.

Healing comes from *faith!* It is God who heals! Is it the faith of the individual or the faith of the one doing the anointing that heals? James says to let them pray over the sick person, anointing him/her with oil and then the prayer of faith will save the sick. It is the faith of both. The one comes in faith to be healed, yet the one carrying out the anointing also has faith in God, the great Healer. That is exactly why and how I anoint the sick, calling in prayer for God to come and heal the sick in the mighty name of Jesus Christ. In the name of Jesus Christ because Christ says in John14:13-15, "*And whatsoever ye shall ask in my name, that will I do, that the Father may be glorified in the Son. If ye shall ask any thing in my name, I will do* it. *If ye love me, keep my commandments.*"

This is a promise from Christ Himself. If I/we ask anything in His name, He will do it. Then He goes on to add if we love Him, we keep His commandments. When I and Pastor Godfrey Mugolo anointed with oil, laid hands on and prayed for new converts who were physically sick the people saw healings taking place immediately. That was nothing of us, but it was all of God. I will cover this subject in another chapter. We shared with them the good news of Christ who loved them and gave His life that they might live. Not only live but go free from the bondage of satan and his workers of iniquity, witches, and witch doctors. The people were living under a black cloud of fear. But fear paralyzes people into doing nothing, and the fear is transparent on their face and transmits to those around. Christ broke those chains of captivity on the cross. By giving their life to Christ He would set the sinner free. They were prisoners to sin and death, but Christ set the captives free. When these poor souls cried out to God for Salvation and received forgiveness God took them into His family. He put a new song in their mouth and they too could sing of a truth the hymn, "Thank God I Am Free."

For a long time I travelled
Down a long lonely road;
My heart was so heavy in sin I sank low.
Then I heard about Jesus,
What a wonderful hour;
I'm so glad that I found out
He could bring me out
Through His saving power.

Chorus:
Thank God I am free, free, free
From this world of sin.
I've been washed in the blood of Jesus,
I've been born again.
Hallelujah, I'm saved, saved, saved
By His wonderful grace.
I'm so glad that I found out
He could bring me out
And show me the way.

Like a bird out of prison
That has taken its flight;
Like a blind man that God
Gave back his sight.
Like a poor wretched beggar
That's found fortune and fame,
I'm so glad that I found out
He could bring me out
Thro' His holy name.

Recorded by Carroll Roberson
Written by James McFall

One night I was preaching in a church in Northern Ireland. I had the anointing of God upon me and there were things being spoken that I had not prepared but I knew God was moving. At the end of the meeting I gave the invitation for those who knew not Christ but were burdened with sin to give their life to Christ. There were two people who I had the privilege to lead to Christ, but I was very aware of a young lady in the gathering. Throughout the meeting she appeared uncomfortable and restless. The Holy Spirit prompted me to ask if anyone needed to talk to me privately to come forward.

The young lady did not move but when I had finished praying, she rose quickly to leave. I stepped down from the pulpit and went quickly after her to the door. I smiled at her and asked if I may speak with her for a moment. She dropped her head but waited. Taking her aside I said that I felt led to speak with her about her life and was I correct in saying she was serving the devil. She still never spoke so I went on and told her the Holy Spirit was showing me she was a child of the devil and was involved in Ouija boards and the occult. As I continued to share what I was being shown by the Holy Spirit she started to cry and told me how she was tormented day and night by demons and could not get peace. She could not tell anyone because she was brought up to go to church and people had this good opinion of her. To tell them would cause her to lose her self-respect. Again, I told her the only answer was Jesus Christ and He alone could save her and set her free.

I explained that nothing was too hard for God and she was not beyond redemption. Furthermore, Christ loved her and died for her and He was standing with open arms to take her in to become a child of God in the family of God. Christ would deliver her from her captors and set her free as free as a bird. This young lady cried out to God and God heard her cry and delivered her. Not only did she have faith to believe in her Salvation but faith to believe she was set free and her past was all forgiven. The tears of repentance turned to tears of joy and I told her to go and tell others what Christ had done for her. She could sing with assurance the hymn, "Thank God I am free."

When anyone prays the prayer of true repentance which I and others refer to as the 'sinner's prayer' it is not the words that are used; not the person who is leading in prayer but by faith alone that saves the poor lost sinner. The young lady was indeed as free as a bird and yet again Christ demonstrated His love for the lost and the power in His Blood shed at Calvary so that you and I might be saved.

Does my life reflect Christ? It should because I may be the only bible some people will read. I want my prayer to always be: "Let them see Christ in me Lord." If they do see Christ in me, they will believe and trust Christ as their Saviour and be saved. That is my ultimate goal – souls won for Jesus Christ, the KING of Kings, the LORD of Lords, and the heavenly kingdom of God extended. Instead of using cosmetic toners to look good, let me strive and ask God to give me spiritual toner so that I will be a reflection of Christ and reflect His character.

It matters not whether in Africa, the United Kingdom, the Americas, Pakistan, India, or anywhere else in the world. It is the same God I speak about, it is the same Gospel message I bring, and the same Blood of Jesus Christ which still washes a sinner's heart as white as snow. Our God never changes. He is: "*Jesus Christ the same yesterday, and to day, and for ever.*" Hebrew 13:8. Glory to His matchless name. This is the God I serve. He is awesome in might and in power and in strength. You and I try to fit God into a box, but we tend to forget He is the God who created the universe, the galaxies the heavens above, and the earth below. He even created you and me. My God is a big God and can do anything.

7. God will take us up

When we live according to the Scriptures, we will have nothing to fear when the 'upper-taker' comes for us should that be in death if the rapture of the Church does not take place before that. Why should I concern myself about an undertaker coming? Because I am a child of God and I know for sure I am a child of God; if the angel of death were to visit me my soul would leave this body and go to be with the Lord. Absent from the body and present with the Lord. Like David said in Psalm 23:4, "*Yea, though I walk through the valley of the shadow of death, I will fear no evil: for thou* art *with me.*" Death is only a shadow and I know a shadow of something is not the real thing. A dog can bite but the shadow of a dog cannot bite or harm me. For the child of God, it would not be real death but just a shadow. I would not experience the sting of death. I would long be out of here before an undertaker could be called. When the upper taker comes for me, I know that death will be no big deal. I, myself, everyone alive on this earth should live every day as though Christ could return, or the angel of death could visit at any moment.

The number 7 is the number in Scripture for completion or/and perfection. David (and you and I) was complete in Christ. David was made perfect in weakness.

For us to be complete in Christ there are 7 points we must fulfil.

1. We must wait upon God
2. We must know personally the Salvation of God
3. We must have a solid foundation for our faith — the cross of Jesus Christ
4. We must stand on the solid Rock; depend on Christ to hold us in the palm of His hand
5. We will have a new song in our mouth our God to magnify
6. We will desire to be like Jesus so people will see Jesus reflected in our countenance
7. We need not fear the undertaker as God will be our upper-taker

Finally

"Many shall ***see*** it, *and* ***fear****, and shall* ***trust*** *in the LORD."*

We can see three further important points which we will look at under three words: See, fear, trust.

Each person needs to know that they are born in sin and **see** Jesus Christ as the pure and righteous Saviour of the world and so He can become their Saviour too.

They need to **fear** because of their great sin and need of forgiveness.

They need to **trust** Christ as their personal Saviour and become born again.

This is the great truth found in the second part of verse three. Here we have the gospel in a nutshell. I can have confidence in no other because whether in life or in death I am a winner. As Paul says in Scripture, *"For me to live is Christ: to die is gain."* (Philippians 1:21) This is what I believe. This is what I am depending on. This is my confidence.

May I be bold and ask you what are you believing in? What are you depending on and where or in whom have you placed your confidence? As you answer this question honestly before God may I ask you a further question? Is your belief, your dependence and your confidence rightly placed or is it misplaced? As I had to face these questions, so must you, and only you can answer.

What is That in Your Hand?

> "*And Moses answered and said, But, behold, they will not believe me, nor hearken unto my voice: for they will say, The LORD hath not appeared unto thee. And the LORD said unto him, What* is that in thine hand? And he said, A rod. *And he said, Cast it on the ground. And he cast it on the ground, and it became a serpent; and Moses fled from before it. And the LORD said unto Moses, Put forth thine hand, and take it by the tail. And he put forth his hand, and caught it, and it became a rod in his hand:*" Exodus 4:1-4

The highly regarded historian, Josephus, summarised Moses' career in a remarkable sentence: "He had few equals as a general and none as a prophet, to the extent that in all his pronouncements, one seemed to hear the voice of God himself."

Moses: The name means "Drawn Forth, Taken out of the water or a Son."

Moses was the youngest son of Amram and Jochebed, of the family of Kohath. (Exodus 2:10-20; Acts 7:20-38; Hebrews 11:24, 25).

Luke, under the inspiration of God, penned the follow tribute to Moses.

"In which time Moses was born, and was exceeding fair, and nourished up in his father's house three months: And when he was cast out, Pharaoh's daughter took him up, and nourished him for her own son. And Moses was learned in all the wisdom of the Egyptians, and was mighty in words and in deeds. And when he was full forty years old, it came into his heart to visit his brethren the children of Israel. And seeing one of them *suffer wrong, he defended* him, *and avenged him that was oppressed, and smote the Egyptian: For he supposed his brethren would have understood how that God by his hand would deliver them: but they understood not. And the next day he shewed himself unto them as they strove, and would have set them at one again, saying, Sirs, ye are brethren; why do ye wrong one to another? But he that did his neighbour wrong thrust him away, saying, Who made thee a ruler and a judge over us? Wilt thou kill me, as thou diddest the Egyptian yesterday? Then fled Moses at this saying, and was a stranger in the land of Madian, where he begat two sons. And when forty years were expired, there appeared to him in the wilderness of mount Sina an angel of the Lord in a flame of fire in a bush. When Moses saw* it, *he wondered at the sight: and as he drew near to behold* it, *the voice of the Lord came unto him,* Saying, *I* am *the God of thy fathers, the God of Abraham, and the God of Isaac, and the God of Jacob. Then Moses trembled, and durst not behold. Then said the Lord to him, Put off thy shoes from thy feet: for the place where thou standest is holy ground. I have seen, I have seen the affliction of my people which is in Egypt, and I have heard their groaning, and am come down to deliver them. And now come, I will send thee into Egypt. This Moses whom they refused, saying, Who made thee a ruler and a judge? the same did God send* to be *a ruler and a deliverer by the hand of the angel which appeared to him in the bush. He brought*

them out, after that he had shewed wonders and signs in the land of Egypt, and in the Red sea, and in the wilderness forty years. This is that Moses, which said unto the children of Israel, A prophet shall the Lord your God raise up unto you of your brethren, like unto me; him shall ye hear. This is he, that was in the church in the wilderness with the angel which spake to him in the mount Sina, and with *our fathers: who received the lively oracles to give unto us:"* Acts 7:20-38

Verses 31-34 refers directly to Exodus 3:5-10 which reads as follows: *"And he said, Draw not nigh hither: put off thy shoes from off thy feet, for the place whereon thou standest* is *holy ground. Moreover he said, I* am *the God of thy father, the God of Abraham, the God of Isaac, and the God of Jacob. And Moses hid his face; for he was afraid to look upon God. And the LORD said, I have surely seen the affliction of my people which* are *in Egypt, and have heard their cry by reason of their taskmasters; for I know their sorrows; And I am come down to deliver them out of the hand of the Egyptians, and to bring them up out of that land unto a good land and a large, unto a land flowing with milk and honey; unto the place of the Canaanites, and the Hittites, and the Amorites, and the Perizzites, and the Hivites, and the Jebusites. Now therefore, behold, the cry of the children of Israel is come unto me: and I have also seen the oppression wherewith the Egyptians oppress them. Come now therefore, and I will send thee unto Pharaoh, that thou mayest bring forth my people the children of Israel out of Egypt."*

Verse 37 quotes Deuteronomy 18:15:*"The Lord thy God will raise up unto thee a Prophet from the midst of thee, of thy brethren, like unto me; unto him ye shall hearken;"* Moses had prophesied that the Messiah would come, and it happened exactly as Moses said.

The writer to the Hebrews, commonly believed to be Paul the Apostle, in chapter 11 added Moses to the list of greats. This chapter can be named, 'The roll call in the Hall of Fame.'

> *"By faith Moses, when he was born, was hid three months of his parents, because they saw he was a proper child; and they were not afraid of the king›s commandment. By faith Moses, when he was come to years, refused to be called the son of Pharaoh›s daughter; Choosing rather to suffer affliction with the people of God, than to enjoy the pleasures of sin for a season; Esteeming the reproach of Christ greater riches than the treasures in Egypt: for he had respect unto the recompense of the reward. By faith he forsook Egypt, not fearing the wrath of the king: for he endured, as seeing him who is invisible. Through faith he kept the passover, and the sprinkling of blood, lest he that destroyed the firstborn should touch them."*
> Hebrews 11:23-28

This great Hebrew leader was born at a time the king of Egypt had resolved to kill every newborn male child among the Israelites. We know the story of how Pharaoh's daughter rescued the baby Moses from the water and adopted him as her own son. Moses was to be reared a royal and then to become the deliverer of his people.

The leadership skills God gave Moses was outstanding. It is important to note that he learned leadership principles and faith from his parents (Exodus18:23) and he learned leadership principles and organization from his father-in-law, Jethro (Exodus 18:13-27). Moses was an able learner and becomes an able leader with great leadership characteristics.

God is wisdom and in having that, He did not just tell Moses to go and lead a people, but you and I can see how He put Moses into a family of leadership. This family was the very best in the world at that time. God enabled Moses to then take what he had learned and use the good of it to lead his people. God is always away ahead of us and is working things out according to His plan and purpose.

Hebrews 11 lists Moses in that great list of the faithful and describes the leadership characteristics that allowed him to succeed in the immense task given to him by the Lord. Decisions must be made even if they involve fear and risk. Moses made the decision to forsake Egypt (Israel's security) and leave for the Promised Land (God's security). But getting from man's security to God's real security was through the wilderness. The same for me and you, to get to God's security inevitably takes us through the wilderness which tests our faith in God. It takes real Spiritual leaders to lead the way even in the face of opposition. Moses was to further realise this, as opposition came continually and strongly, but He remained a Godly leader throughout.

Now it is one thing to decide and another thing to do. When Moses was negotiating Israel's release from Egypt with Pharaoh, he pronounced the plagues one by one to Egypt. When it came to the Passover, Moses led Israel to be obedient to the observance even in a strange land because it was right. By faith they passed through the Red Sea as by dry land: which the Egyptians attempting to do were drowned.

When God says move, it's time to move. It is the responsibility of Spiritual leaders to lead God's people through the Red Seas of life. The sea is in front of us; the mountains are on either side of us; and the enemy is closing in behind us. God says He will open up the sea and give us dry passage to the other side. It is time to move out and real leaders with the leadership characteristics of Moses will lead God's people to the other side.

It is no wonder that most Jews, Christians, and other religions alike consider Moses one of the most able leaders of all time. He was a great spiritual leader who embodied the great leadership characteristics listed in the Bible. But of course, the leadership characteristics of Christ and His teaching on faith overshadows all of them. (Hebrews 12:1-3)

God moves in a mysterious way
His wonders to perform;
He plants His footsteps in the sea
And rides upon the storm.
William Cooper (1774)

There are many titles we may give to Moses, such as, leader, statesman, historian, even prophet but the greatest honour bestowed on him was the privilege of being called, 'The friend of God.' What an intimacy he enjoyed with God and the good news... you and I can have that same relationship. How do I know this for me and you? Because in Acts 10:34 Peter states; *"Of a truth I perceive that God is no respecter of persons:"* What God is saying through Peter that the gospel is for everyone, of every nation, of every colour, and every race, Jew and Gentile, poor, middle class, and royalty.

Moses lived for 120 years (Deuteronomy 34:7) and it is interesting to note that his life was equally divided into 3 periods of forty years each. The first forty years was from his birth until he had to flee into Midian. (Exodus 2:15; Acts 7:23) We could say of this period as Pharaoh's son he was a 'somebody.'

The second period of forty years was from the time he took flight into Midian until the Exodus. (Acts 7:30) This time he spent in the desert and he learned very quickly how to become a 'nobody.' It takes time spent in the backside of the desert to bring one from a 'somebody' to a 'nobody'. I proved this in my 10 years following the stroke and being plunged into a desert experience.

The third forty years from the Exodus until his death (Numbers 14:33) we see him as a leader of God's people, and this was when he was to prove God was 'Everybody'. This he proved when He spoke with God face to face. God was to be his very best friend.

One other thing I want to highlight about Moses is how Moses is a type of Christ. Let me explain how this is. These are the points of similarity:

1. Both were preserved from death at birth.

Moses was left by his mother in a reed basket on the river Nile and was rescued by Pharaoh's daughter and raised in the palace despite Pharaoh's decree that all Hebrew children were to be killed at birth. (Exodus 2:2-10)

Christ was born in Bethlehem in Judea during the reign of King Herod. Herod, when he heard that Jesus was born 'King of the Jews', was disturbed and when he was outwitted by the wise men, he decreed that all baby boys under two years of age be killed. God sent an angel to warn Joseph of Herod's decree and told him to flee to Egypt and remain there until the Lord told him it was safe to return. (Mathew 2:14-18)

2. Both were tempted but were masters over temptation.

Moses was tempted by Pharaoh. "*Then Pharaoh also called*

the wise men and the sorcerers: now the magicians of Egypt, they also did in like manner with their enchantments. For they cast down every man his rod, and they became serpents: but Aaron's rod swallowed up their rods." Exodus 7:11-12

Christ was tempted by the devil. *"Then was Jesus led up of the spirit into the wilderness to be tempted of the devil."* Matthew 4:1

3. Both knew what it meant to fast for 40 days.
   Moses - Exodus 34:28, Christ - Mathew 4:2

4. Both had power to control the sea.
   Moses - Exodus 14:21, Christ - Mathew 8:26

5. Both fed a multitude.
   Moses - Exodus 16:15, Christ - Mathew 14:20,21

6. Both had to endure a murmuring and complaining people.
   Moses - Exodus 15:24, Christ - Mark 7:2

7. Both were not recognised in their home country.
   Moses - Numbers 12:1, Christ - John 7:5

8. Both were mighty prayer warriors.
   Moses - Exodus 32:32, Christ - John 17:9

9. Both spoke as the oracles of God.
   Moses - Deuteronomy 18:18, Christ - Deuteronomy 18:18 also looks to Christ who was yet to come but Christ fulfilled this prophecy, John 8:26; 12:49; 14:10; 17:8

10. Both had seventy helpers.
    Moses - Numbers 11:16-17, Christ - Luke 10:1

11. Both established memorials.
    Moses - Exodus 12:14, Christ - Luke 22:19

12. Both reappeared after death.
    Moses - Mathew 17:3, Christ - Acts 1:3

Moses gave us the first five books of the bible which are known in Greek as 'The Pentateuch'; the Jews call it the 'Torah' which has 24 books of which five of them are: Genesis, Exodus, Leviticus, Numbers, and Deuteronomy. When Jesus spoke and said, *"Moses spoke of me,"* He set his seal on the books and the authorship of these books. Moses died on the plain of Moab. God called Moses, his servant, to climb the lonely mountain of Nebo. When Moses arrived at the top of the mountain he was kissed to sleep by the angels and God buried him.

> *"So Moses the servant of the LORD died there in the land of Moab, according to the word of the LORD. And he buried him in a valley in the land of Moab, over against Beth-peor: but no man knoweth of his sepulchre unto this day."* Deuteronomy 34:5-6

He was the only man in the bible to have God as his undertaker. The Scripture tells us, *"And Moses was an hundred and twenty years old when he died: his eye was not dim, nor his natural force abated."*

Moses was a great man, but not a perfect one. Before his death Moses delivered his final sermon, known to us as the book of Deuteronomy. It was following this sermon that Moses climbed the peak, Pisgah, on the mountain of Nebo. There has never been another prophet in Israel like Moses, as a mediator between God and man. (Acts 3:17-26 and Hebrews 3) Moses is mentioned in the New Testament more than any other Old Testament figure. He appeared at Jesus' transfiguration. Moses was used of God right up into his old age and till death. This gives me great hope and that also gives great hope to you or anyone reading this that is well on in years and still questions if God can use you. Perhaps you are feeling that you are a nobody and could not speak to someone who society would consider in a higher class to you. Well God can use you to fulfil His plans regardless of what man may say or think. Let me share my own personal example here.

Training for Reigning

I was born a farmer's daughter and therefore considered a country girl. A country girl is not born with the proverbial silver spoon in her mouth but has to work hard for a living. I was and still am a country girl at heart and was brought up to work hard. I never aspired to stand before Royalty or the upper class of society, but God had different ideas.

When I was pursuing my career there was much learning and training involved. For example, when I was meeting with government representatives who were visiting from Korea, I had to do my research before the meeting to know the protocol I would be expected to observe. On the first meeting I should not proceed to shake hands but instead extend my business card to the visitor. To have gone to shake hands would have been extremely rude even derogatory.

This later extended to meeting Prime Ministers, Ambassadors, and even Princes. Little did I know then that this training in my career would become very useful later in my life? God makes no mistakes and my work was to be my training ground for entrance to the next level. Then God opened the door. How good was that?

No one can stumble into going before royals and I was no different. I was soon to see the hand of God again and how He had provided the opportunity through my earlier training.

On my second visit to Uganda I was given an invitation to visit a prince and his family in Kampala. I was taken to this very grand residence that was not visible to the outside world. When the electric doors opened back staff escorted me in and presented me to the prince and his wife and his brothers who were also princes. The opulence was stark in comparison to the humble huts and small houses I was acquainted with. There was a grand table and chairs furnished with brass ornamental work. A large television was in the corner of the family room and the rest of the furnishings oozed riches and wealth. The prince introduced me to the rest of his family, and I was ushered through to the grand dining room where the table was laid for a meal. In any of the nations I have visited in Africa it is the normal procedure before you are invited to eat that the lady brings a basin, soap, and a jug of water. I would hold my hands over the basin, and she would pour some water over my hands. I would then soap them and scrub well and she would pour water over my hand until all the soap was gone and hands were clean. Not so on this visit; there was a small tap and basin over to a corner of the room where I was invited to wash my hands under warm water from the tap. Then I was given a clean towel for my use only. Up until this I was used shaking the surplus water of my hands and to be content.

The prince did almost all the talking, asking me about my reason for being in Uganda. As I started to share my testimony with him, he quickly interrupted me to say that they were all of the Roman Catholic faith. When I finished sharing my testimony, he asked me if God would not allow them into Heaven because of all the good works they did and also, they were good living. Sadly, I have heard this statement many times, and often been asked the same questions so it was time to tell them what God said on the matter. I turned in my Bible to Ephesians 2:8,9; *"For by grace are ye saved through faith; and that not of yourselves: it is the gift of God: Not of works, lest any man should boast."*

This is a concise summary of how a person is saved. It is a cardinal tenet of the Gospel that people are made righteous through trust in Christ rather than through their own merit. Salvation is for those who trust Christ alone to save them. As a result, you and I can't boast about it. Good works comes as a result of me loving Christ for saving me. This is similar to my relationship with my husband. Because of his love for me and me for him, he chose to marry me. As a result of my deep love for my husband I choose to do all I can to make him feel happy and loved. If I do something that hurts his feelings, I seek to make restitution as quickly as possible. It is the very same in the spiritual. Because of Christ's great love for me, I repented of all my sinful life, choosing instead to live my life for Christ. Therefore, it follows that I will do my utmost, by God's grace given to me, to obey God's word and be obedient in all I do.

The next profound statement he made on behalf of his family was that they prayed regularly through the Virgin Mary to God. Again, this is a common belief especially with people of the Roman Catholic faith. This is what they are erroneously taught by the priests. However, the Word of God is the final Word on all things and it states clearly in 1Timothy 2:5, 6: *"For there is one God, and one mediator between God and men, the man Christ Jesus; Who gave himself a ransom for all..."*

It is sad when I meet someone who is blinded by the errors of their Catholic faith, but it is even worse when I meet Protestants who are equally blinded. You may wonder at my stating this but here in the United Kingdom there is open access to the bible for all Protestants which are not so readily permitted for the Catholics. I meet Protestants who believe that because they were born into a Protestant home and sent to Sunday school and church, they have got all that is necessary for Heaven's door to open and let them in. We have seen many, many, years of terrorist fighting in our wee land; terrorist from both so called Protestant and Catholic faiths. I do not believe for one moment that the terrorist who were fighting under the banner 'For God and Ulster' knew or had a personal relationship with Jesus Christ. I recall talking with some of them and asking them did they know God. It was the same answer always; they knew of God and believed there was a God out there, but they did not know God or were able to talk with God.

Knowing about or acknowledging there is a God somewhere does not do anything for a stony heart. A personal and close relationship with Jesus Christ after asking Him to be Lord and Saviour of my life and of yours will remove that stony heart and put a new heart that oozes the love of God. When I have the love of God oozing from my heart, I want to see men and woman come to know Jesus Christ as Saviour and to turn from their wicked way. I do not wish to see them killed. Only God can carry out this heart transplant in a life.

It matters not what faith you and I claim to hold unto; what colour our skin may be or what denomination we claim to be a member of. In the Kingdom of God there is neither Protestant or Catholic, Jew or Greek, black or white, red or brown. All titles must be dropped because in heaven there is only one title and that is 'The KING of Kings and LORD of Lords'. Jesus Christ is KING!

You and I have direct access to the throne of God through Jesus Christ our Lord. And this is exactly as I shared it with the royal family. It is a fundamental doctrine of the Christian faith. When my time of visiting was coming to an end the prince surprised me by asking if I would pray for his mother who was very elderly and unwell. I was pleased to be asked as it meant I did not have to initiate the request, but I really wished to pray in the home. The prince's wife went and brought in her mother-in-law and seated her beside me. She spoke warmly to me and seemed genuinely pleased I was there and would indeed pray. The prince, himself, suffered from ulcers on his feet and he requested prayer for healing. After praying and extending my gratitude for being allowed to visit and share a meal in their home I took my leave.

Friend, I could barely take it in that I had been before princes and been afforded the opportunity to both share my personal testimony and explain the Gospel of Jesus Christ at length. Only my God could do something amazing like that. Only God Himself could make a way for a wee country girl like me to stand before princes and give me the ability to share the Word and truth of God. Only God could empower me with the strength and words to address royalty. In Matthew 10:18, Christ is speaking, and He states, "*And ye shall be brought before governors and kings for my sake, for a testimony against them and the Gentiles.*"

What is meant here is to take the opportunity to witness to those high in government and to royalty because the time will come when it will not be acceptable, nor will it be tolerated for the gospel to be shared or preached. But high society will have no excuse. I had to use the opportunity given to me by the Lord to tell this royal family their need of Salvation. I am accountable to God for every opportunity given to me to speak about Christ and I must always discharge my responsibility.

You cannot change the past, but you will ruin the present by worrying about the future.

When my life and yours is owned by God, whatever you and I use for Him becomes His property. In the life of Moses, it was his rod.

A rod — Most commentators regard the 'rod' of Moses as his shepherd's crook, and this is certainly possible; but the etymology of the word employed seems rather to point to an ordinary staff, or walking-stick. Egyptians of rank usually carried long *batons;* and one suggestion is that the rod of Moses was "that which he had been accustomed to carry as the son of Pharaoh's daughter." But even if this was still in his possession after forty years of exile, he is not likely to have taken it with him when he went a-shepherding. Probably the rod was a common staff, such as a shepherd of eighty years old might need for a support.

Verse 4: ***Take it by the tail*** — Those who venture to handle poisonous snakes, like the modern Egyptians and the inhabitants of the coast of Barbary, generally take hold of them by the neck, in which case they are unable to bite. To test the faith and courage of Moses, the command is given him to lay hold of *this* serpent "by the tail."

He put forth his hand — Faith triumphed over instinct. Moses had fled from the snake when first he saw it (Exodus 4:3). Now he is daring enough to stoop down, put his hand on the creature's tail, and so lift it up.

It became a rod —Its real nature returned to it. Once more it was, not a stiffened serpent, but an actual staff, or walking-stick.

"And the Lord said to Moses, put forth thy hand, and take it by the tail..." Which to do might seem most dangerous, since it might turn upon him and bite him. This was ordered,

partly that Moses might be assured it was really a serpent, and not in appearance only; and partly to try his courage. It suggested to him, that he need not be afraid of it, it would not hurt him. I believe that he is commanded to take it by the tail, for to meddle with the serpent's head belonged not to Moses, but to God that spoke to him out of the bush:

Moses, sweltering in the heat of the Sinai desert, is engaged in a pity party. "I can't do what you want, Lord, because of this excuse and that excuse. People won't accept me. I can't talk good. Let somebody else do it."

But arguing with God is never a good idea. You and I don't win. Even if you and I say "no" (and God may let us), you and I lose. When you and I say "no" or "I can't," we miss out on the great adventure God has for us when we are in the centre of His will for your life and mine. But what is that will?

In the barren wastes of the Sinai, God asks Moses a simple question: *"What's in your hand?"* Moses is a shepherd. That's all he's done for forty years, and he's ready to retire at age 80. "What's in your hand, Moses?"

Moses looks at his hand. "A staff," he tells God — as if God didn't know.

The Lord says, "Throw it on the ground." Moses does so, and it becomes a snake. God tells him to pick it up by the tail and it turns back into a staff. Over the next forty years of Moses' life, God uses that simple wooden stick to deliver the Israelites from Pharaoh, to open the Red Sea, to win a battle with the Amalekites, to bring water from a rock. Who would have thought? As Moses learns to use in faith what God has put in his hand, his life is changed — as well as the course of world history.

Without rebuke the Lord gave Moses two pieces of counsel. One related to His person; the other related to His work. He told Moses who He was, and then He told him what He was going to do. Also, the order in that expression is as important as the facts themselves.

He repeated the message from the burning bush, saying, "I am" five times in Exodus chapter 6.

"And God said to Moses, "I am Yahweh—'the LORD.' I appeared to Abraham, to Isaac, and to Jacob as El-Shaddai—'God Almighty'—but I did not reveal my name, Yahweh, to them." (Exodus 6:2-3 NLT)

- I am the Lord.... verse 2, 'Yahweh'
  Meaning 'The Lord' – The only living and true God.
- I am the Lord....verse 6
- I am the Lord....verse 7
- I am the Lord....verse 8
- I am the Lord....verse 29

Repeatedly the Lord keeps telling Moses to stop looking at others. He was saying that Moses had his eyes on the wrong place but instead he was to get his eyes back on the Lord. God was saying to Moses and He says to me and you also, "Remember who I am!"

Turn your eyes upon Jesus,
Look full in His wonderful face
And the things of earth will grow strangely dim
In the light of His glory and grace.
(Helen H. Lemmel, 1922. *Public Domain)*

The Lord knows exactly what He is doing in my life and I just must stop being stubborn and listen. When God gave me gifts, they were for a reason and though I kept looking at the physical God was saying to me to look on Him for that is where my strength comes from. Because of who God is, that is why He does the very best in my life and I must recognise and keep this foremost in my mind when difficult times come.

Just as God commanded Moses, He was also saying what would happen, and how Moses was to be part of this. Moses was not to fear because God was in control. When God speaks that is often when it is most difficult for me because that is when he is asking me to do something that I would rather not to do. When God told me to take the Gospel to Uganda I did not drop all and go. No! I hesitated, and in my hesitation, I was actually saying I did not trust God. How could God want me to go to Africa? Who was I kidding besides myself? I did more than hesitate I actually refused in the belief it could not be God's will. Has God spoken to you and asked you to give Him your life and He will forgive you and be your Saviour and Friend? Has God asked you to give of yourself, of your possessions, of your time or of your talent to support and do a work for Him? Only you can answer that as I had to answer for myself, but God will never ask you to give, do, or go somewhere without Him giving you the grace to do so. I was soon to learn what God could do with my life fully surrendered to Him.

Paul says when writing to the Corinthians in 1Corinthians 1:27; *"But God hath chosen the foolish things of the world to confound the wise; and God hath chosen the weak things of the world to confound the things which are mighty;"*

God did not choose philosophers, or orators, or statesmen or men of wealth, and power, and interest in the world, to publish the gospel of grace and peace. Rather He chose the lowly, weak, and ordinary people to serve the purposes of His glory. Though not many noble are usually called by Divine grace, there have been some down through the years, who have not been ashamed of the gospel of Christ. Persons of every rank, class, and creed stand in need of pardoning grace. Often, a humble Christian though poor in this world's goods, has more true knowledge of the gospel, than those who have made the letter of Scripture the study of their lives, but who have studied it rather as the witness of men, than as the word of God. Even young children have gained knowledge of the Divine truths of God as to be able to silence the mockers and infidels. The reason is, they are taught of God. The purpose in all this is that no flesh should glory in His presence.

When God had called me first it was through my reading and studying of Jeremiah 1:4-9: *"Then the word of the LORD came unto me, saying, Before I formed thee in the belly I knew thee; and before thou camest forth out of the womb I sanctified thee, and I ordained thee a prophet unto the nations. Then said I, Ah, Lord GOD! behold, I cannot speak: for I am a child. But the LORD said unto me, Say not, I am a child: for thou shalt go to all that I shall send thee, and whatsoever I command thee thou shalt speak. Be not afraid of their faces: for I am with thee to deliver thee, saith the LORD. Then the LORD put forth his hand, and touched my mouth. And the LORD said unto me, Behold, I have put my words in thy mouth."*

In this I, like Jeremiah, learned three important truths about God:

1. God's knowledge of all things including individuals like me.
2. God's ability to choose individuals for specific tasks even before they come into existence.
3. God's willingness to extend His authority to the people He calls.

God set Jeremiah apart to perform a special task and that was to be a prophet for God to the nation of Israel. I was soon aware that I too, was set apart for a special work for the Lord. When God had me in design, before my mother and father had thought of me, He knew exactly the plans He had for my life. When I prayed and asked God to show me what those plans were, I never thought He would ask me to travel and take the Gospel to foreign lands. All I could say to myself and to God; there was no way I would or could do such a task. However, just as God answered Jeremiah when he said he could not possibly do such a task and God told him to not look at the flesh but to trust his God who would teach him and empower him for the job, so God was saying to me, 'Eileen, look beyond yourself to the importance of the task I am calling you to do.' I had to meet God's requirement for me to serve the Lord which included obedience. I had to do what the Lord was asking me to do in total faith.

The Price of the High Calling

I had to be willing to travel even if that meant at a cost that I could not afford in the natural but to trust God to supply the money to meet the need. It also would mean coping with strange foods and very basic accommodation. Then there would be the faithful delivery of the Lord's message regardless of who I stood in front of. God promised to put the word in my mouth giving me the assurance of being able to speak authoritatively in public. He would have to because there was no way I had the ability or the inclination to do this kind of public speaking. Like Jeremiah I Knew I would be ridiculed, condemned, hated, and even threatened but God would be with me as long as I was obedient. Had I the faith?

If I stepped out in faith to fulfil the ministry God was calling me to do, I would know for sure that my faith in action would be followed by God's blessings on all aspects of my life. God alone would meet the needs financially. I would not ask anyone but my Lord for money. God would keep me fed regardless of my likes and dislikes of the food provided. Also, God would be my shelter when I would sleep in sparse surroundings. My great God was all I needed. Did I have enough faith to go the journey? Would I step out of the 'boat' so to speak and then start to sink or would I 'walk' on the water with Christ as my 'lifeguard'?

However, I chose to take the easy route and follow my head. I thought I could please God by witnessing around my community; I would not travel to a foreign and unknown land. I had forgotten who was in control of my life and it was not me. God kept speaking. It was that continual witness to my conscious and senses that eventually I gave in and surrendered to the will of God. One day I just could not go any further and I cried out to God and said, "Lord I am willing to go. I have no idea how and no idea why You are asking me. I do not understand why You want me. It is all so impossible for me; I have nothing, but what I have I give totally to You. You will have to do all the work in and through me because I am nothing Lord. I am wholly trusting You, Lord, for I have no other."

Thank God He was in control. When I surrendered to the Lord, the immediate peace I felt was so immense. Over the next days and weeks, I watched His plan and purpose unfold in my life.

One thing I needed to learn was to trust in time of trial. God knows how it will all fit together even in times when I could not imagine how it could possibly happen. Even when something seemed to be a negative for me, later I was to learn that it was all in God's greater plan. One of these amazing insights I was to learn about afterwards. As I stated earlier, I had my major stroke in April 2004. God was carving out my future in the ministry with who He was planning to partner me with. That was when God had called Pastor Godfrey Mugolo into the ministry and Godfrey was also commencing his training to become a pastor. Now you will have to agree that was not a coincidence. My future partner in the ministry was starting to train at the exact time God was pulling me out of my career and preparing me for His ministry. That is the work of the Lord. Then ten years later God opened the door for both of us to meet and minister together.

From Praise to Partner

I remember that day with great fondness. I arrived at a little church on the edge of Kampala, Uganda, on the Sunday morning and was led up to the platform and offered a seat alongside the pastor. When I lifted my head and looked straight ahead my eyes rested on this lovely young man playing the keyboard. He gave me a big broad smile and continued playing as the congregation sang lovely hymns in praise and worship to God. When it was time for the sermon I was introduced and called forward to preach. The nerves were very evident, and I was sure everyone could see my hands shaking. It was good there was a pulpit to hold.

Imagine my surprise when this young man (Pastor Godfrey Mugolo) got up from behind the keyboard, lifted a microphone, came along side me, and started to interpret. Remembering that English is not a first language I was further amazed to hear he was very fluent in English. He was so fast interpreting, too, that he made me feel relaxed and my nerves left me immediately. This was the first of a close friendship that was to develop into a family relationship and this young man becoming our second son. I will share more about this young man later but enough said to prove how God works. God allowed this divine appointment and we must thank God for it. I did not know then that the young man was an ordained pastor, nor did I know just how or in what way Pastor Godfrey would become so integral a part of my life and ministry.

The Lord went on to tell Moses eight times what He would do:

- See what I will do.... verse 1
- I will bring.... verse 6

- I will deliver.... verse 6
- I will redeem.... verse6
- I will take.... verse 7
- I will be.... verse 7
- I will bring.... verse 8
- I will give.... verse 8

What this says to me is simple. The Lord is saying because He is God and "I am who I am" He will do what is best for me. That is enough for me to go on. That is enough for me to depend on. By reading and understanding what God did for Moses I can take the same promises for myself. After all, God is the same yesterday, today, and forever, so knowing that, I can depend on God for His plan and purpose for my life. I can totally depend on Him equipping, leading, guiding, and protecting me for the tasks ahead. After God told Moses what He was going to do God went on to tell Moses He must believe it. That is what God did to me and that is what God does with you and everyone. So often this is my weakest point in my faith but that is where things are decided; a battle is won or lost. I pray continually, "Lord, I believe, help thou mine unbelief. I must not retreat from the battle. I will not retreat from the battle. I will fight on and even though the storms are mighty, and I am battered I will still believe that You will deliver me; You will bring me through, and I will not drown in the stress and pressures that are being heaped upon me."

The Practical Costs Involved

When God called me to go to Africa and I surrendered to the call, there was much to be considered. The first thing I needed to look at carefully was the invitation extended to me. Was this of God or was it just a pastor's desire and God was not opening the door? When I received the first invitation, I asked the pastor and his church to pray as I and my husband would pray. If God wanted me to go, He would make it abundantly clear and open the way. I had been praying and one Sunday morning I asked God to speak to me clearly through the sermon preached. That morning as the pastor was preaching; he looked down over the congregation and when his eyes were looking my way he stopped and asked, "Are you here this morning and God has been asking you to get up and go and serve Him somewhere that is out of your comfort zone? Have you been given an invitation to share the gospel with others in a foreign land and you are hesitating? Stop procrastinating and go and serve God. Stop you being disobedient to God." That was like a sword cutting into my spirit. I knew the message was for me. On the drive home from church I asked my husband, Ian, what he thought of the sermon. He looked at me with a smile and said, "I think you have got your answer from God loud and clear. What are you going to do now?" I laughed and said, "God wins. I will ring the pastor and confirm I will travel to Uganda later this year."

There was also a need for me to carry out some research into the country I would visit. What was the weather and temperature I would experience? What were the customs and religions; what was the common mode of transport; what was expected of me with regards to protocol; were there any legal standard I was required to meet; what were the health risks and would I need any vaccinations; would I be able to drink the water without adverse reaction; what foods could I eat and what should I avoid and how should I dress? This was quite a list to research and find answers to and would take much time.

One of my concerns initially was raising the money to pay for my flights. But this was not my major concern. As I began to research about my trip, I soon was to learn that buying tickets was not my only large outlay. There was insurance required but the major surprise of all financials was the vaccinations required by law before I could travel.

I have a wonderful niece, Dorothy McAlister, who is not only a fully qualified nurse with loads of experience, but she also was the top student of her year when graduating in tropical diseases. I spoke with her and she made out a list of all the vaccinations required and put me in touch with her colleague in Lisburn Travel clinic. These vaccination injections I received over a number of weeks so that I would be cleared for travel on my due date. The injections were painless, but the cost was a different matter. Including my Yellow Fever certificate, anti-malaria tablets, and antibiotics, the medication was more costly even than my tickets. I knew now what it was to be totally depending on God. Week by week I was trusting God for the money and sure enough the Lord provided.

Uganda, I learned, is known as *"The Pearl of Africa"* and no small wonder. It has the great river Nile flowing through it including the Great Nile falls. There is also a tremendous wildlife and safari area which a section of the river Nile flows through. There are many tribes in Uganda, and each speaks their own language. Unemployment is rife and poverty abounds right across the nation. Corruption is the norm, and life is cheap. The main religions are Islam, Roman Catholic, and witchcraft. These people need to hear the message of God's saving grace through Jesus Christ dying on the cross to save the people from their sins. I was also to learn that when most 'whites' travelled to Uganda they stayed in the cities but did not travel to the villages because they did not want to compromise on their standard of living. They wanted clean beds, running water, and flush toilets. I knew God was sending me to take His message to the villages. How could these people come to be saved if they never were told? I had to go there but it would be at a great cost.

When I did arrive and travel to the villages it was to stay in sparse dwellings and to sleep on a shallow mattress laid out on the earthen floor. Many times, chicken would be in and out and even a wee kid was to be a regular visitor. I could cope with this but when it came to toileting and washing that was difficult. Usually washing took place outside and some of the 'wash rooms' had no roof and the walls were only barely four foot in height. There was an opening to go in through and to a blanket that was ripped and torn in many places could be used to drape over the opening. Inside the wash area I would find a jerry can filled with cold water and a plastic basin to pour out water to bathe in. Bathing was a carefully executed exercise for me to ensure that I kept my modesty. Washing my hair and bathing in cold water was not a problem because the heat even in early morning was still exceptionally great for me coming from Northern Ireland, thirty degrees and higher was normal. It was great to feel that cool water over my hot body. A few times I have been privileged to say at the home of Pastor Antony Shimenga. To be able to bathe inside a home was a luxury. I often found hot water left in a jerry can with a plastic basin and an enamel mug beside it. I could stand and 'shower' with no thoughts that someone might have a view. I thanked God for these blessings.

When it came to the toilet it was so very difficult for me. I was totally out of my depth. The toilets were all outside and were dry as the toilet was just a hole in the ground. Some had wooden structures over the hole in the ground with a door that did not go near the ground and did not go up to the roof either. Others did not have a roof and still others had only three sides to them so there was no privacy. I confess I struggled with these toilets and I do not think I will ever be comfortable using them. I remember in one place I was staying I went out to use the toilet before retiring to bed for the night. There is no electric in many of the villages and if there are power lines, they will only be in to the main home and not to the out buildings. Even at that the electric is very intermittent. I took my phone for a light to see my way. When I found the toilet and went in the place was crawling with massive cockroaches about two or three times bigger than we would see here at home. I never had seen so many in one place before. I made a quick decision that I was not that desperate for the toilet after all and returned quickly to the house and to bed.

Another time, we had finished a week's mission in a village on the Sunday, after preaching in the third service, Pastor Godfrey and I boarded a couple of motorbikes and travelled for approximately an hour until we reached a town and got a 'taxi' to drive a long distance to our next venue. The motorbikes are known as 'boda bodas' and they are everywhere being used to transport people, children, and cargo. At first, I tried to ride side-saddle as many ladies do out there but was soon to learn it was better to throw a leg over as only then did I feel confident I would not fall off as we negotiated the African roads. These roads I call the 'African massage roads' because as we travel over the humps, bumps, and hollows avoiding massive potholes where possible in the roads it is anything but a smooth journey. The 'taxis' are not the grand vehicles we enjoy in the west. The taxis are minibuses and they are overcrowded beyond belief. The men hang on out through the side door and the best way I can describe my journey is I endured close fellowship and cramped conditions along with the extreme heat in these taxis. We were very glad to use them for transport to enable us to save on expenses and use the money to bless the people and the churches.

I have a major phobia — mice and rats. I can get through with insects and snakes but see a mouse and my blood pressure rockets and my heart rate soars. On this particular Sunday we arrived after midnight to where we were to sleep. After spending weeks without electric it was great to find a light burning in the room. Exhausted and glad to see a bed with clean white sheets I quickly got changed for bed. There was no light switch in my room to turn of the light but being so tired I just went to the bed and lay down. The room was very small, and my bed was against one wall. There was just room for my case laid flat on the floor against the opposite wall with my small knapsack set on top and clear floor space enough to move between for access to the door. I was not concerned in the least and went immediately to sleep. About an hour into my sleep I was awakened knowing something was amiss. I was aware that something had caused me to waken.

I opened my eyes and slowly I turned my head and looked towards my case. Horror of horrors; imagine my consternation and sheer fear when I saw I was not alone; there was a big black rat sitting on my case scraping at my knapsack. God definitely shut my mouth. I did not scream but with a sudden intake of breath I jump up on the middle of the bed and curled up as tight as possible. My heart was pounding. The sweat had broken over me and I was a trembling wreck. I spent the night huddled in the middle of the mattress praying hard, with my eyes open, for God to keep the rat away from me. I was ill!

I am terrified of mice, and rats send me into total paralyses and near mental breakdown. All my family can testify to my strong vocal chords in operation involuntarily when I see a mouse. No one wants to contemplate my reaction to a rat. I still marvel as I recall that night not even muting a sound other than the quick heavy breathing. The Lord was definitely with me and I prayed hard the rest of the night as I kept my vigil for the moves of the rat. When I looked my watch, I had been asleep less than one hour. So much for a good night's sleep then! I was so glad the light was on and I was able to keep a well-lit vigil.

Then another problem arose. How was I to get up and get washed and dressed with a rat in the room? I wanted to run fast. When morning came and God had calmed me down a little, I was afforded the nerve to get washed and dressed. When Pastor Godfrey heard what had taken place his first comment was, "But, Mummy, you never screamed, or I would have come and chased it. I never heard you scream." I told him he had witnessed a miracle – God had shut my mouth. I had the same company every night following that I was staying there. I did not scream during the night, but I did not sleep. It was exhausting days but, seriously, you are probably laughing as you read this, all I can tell you is God undertook for me completely as this was and is not normal behaviour for me.

I was to sleep in this room for several nights and my main thought was how I would cope on my return each night. If this had happened at home, I would have moved to my sister, Dorothy McCullagh's, house until the vermin was killed and all means of their access blocked for all time. I was not in Northern Ireland; I was in Uganda and I was there working for the Lord. I knew I just had to take each night as it came and trust God to keep the vermin from coming unto my bed. It did test my nerves because I still had a 'visitor' each night though not always a rat, but mice and they did like to stay the full night. I survived the stay though a little deprived of sleep.

Another thing I learned in the school of experience was the importance of drinking only bottled water. I was always careful to only drink bottled water until, on one visit to Rwanda; I was given a glass of pure clear water. I had only taken a little drink when I realised it was not bottled water and stopped immediately. It was a Saturday afternoon and by night I was quite ill. On Sunday morning things were no better and I felt weak. I had no breakfast and questioned myself if I was going to be able to preach. My problem was not the sort of thing I wished to share with the people of the host church. In my quiet time I just cried to God to give me strength to deliver the message He had laid on my heart for the people. I sat through all the praise and worship and when called to preach I truly went up in the strength of the Lord. The Lord was with me and I preached without weakness and all glory to God when I gave the invitation for people to give their life to the Lord people responded and souls were saved. It took a further two days before I recovered but was very glad I had prepared for such an eventuality and had medication for the sickness.

When the time comes for travelling into another country the one thing that I have to sort out is to obtain a visa for entry at the border. When I arrive in Entebbe airport in Kampala each time, I must complete a form to obtain a visa for the period of time I plan to remain in the country. This costs money and in Uganda it is approximately $75.00 but at the border of other countries it can be much more or a fraction less. Along with this my cases are carefully and thoroughly searched often at a long table out in the open in front of all the passing public. Even the dirty laundry is checked much to my chagrin. Nothing is easy or straight forward and twice Pastor Godfrey Mugolo and I have lost money to pick pockets at the border between Uganda and Kenya. They are so professional, and it happens fast.

Local customs in Africa are so different from the west and when I encountered some of these for the first time, I was a little embarrassed. When the vehicle pulled up outside the first church I was to visit, a lady came to meet me at the car. As I got out of the car the lady went down on her knees before me and bowed as she reached her hand up to shake my hand. When she stood up, she took my handbag and bible and carried them into the church behind me as I was shown to the front and unto the platform. The lady laid my belongings on the small table in front of me and bowed again before taking her leave.

I learned too that I was not to carry my handbag, bible, and bottle of water at any time even when out walking alone. If there were no ladies around, and that was quite often, one of the men would throw my handbag over his shoulder and whatever else I had along they would carry it, too. When I shared these experiences with my son via social media, he was very quick to reply with a direct message from his father and him – "Mum! Remember it all stops at the airport. Do not be expecting daddy or I to do the same." I can always depend on Derek to give me a reason to laugh.

When it comes to dress, I am always conscious to dress in a manner that does not distract the congregation but brings honour to God. I always wear long frocks and suits with long skirts. Many times, I have worn traditional dress after being gifted frocks by some of the lovely ladies. Standing on high platforms for crusades modesty was always imperative.

These are just a few of the things I was to encounter and require finance for as I served the Lord in Africa. But, do you know something? It is worth it all to see lives changed for God, churches encouraged, and others established, pastors taught, demons cast out, people healed, and practical blessings shared with ladies and children. For some they tell me the cost is too great but when I look at where the Lord has brought me from and what He has done in me nothing is too much. I could never out give the Lord.

As I have written earlier, there was one thing I had learned and that was to take everything to the Lord in prayer and to claim the promises given to me and to present these to the Lord and stand on them. Promises as found in Philippians 4:19 *"But my God shall supply all your need according to His riches in glory by Christ Jesus."* Is it not wonderful to know that you and I can trust that God will always meet our needs? People forget that it is our needs and not our "greeds". I must remember the difference between my wants and my needs. My needs are anything that is necessary to keeping me alive, clothed modestly, and paying my way to meet the laws of the land. Examples of these would be basic staples where food is concerned to keep me nourished and in normal health. My clothes would be what I expect to keep me dressed in a modest and respectable fashion with changes to allow me to do laundry and money to pay for electric, heating fuel, and council taxes. My greeds are the luxuries in life like holidays abroad, extra fashion clothes, and accessories, fancy furnishings for my home, and pampering for a feel-good factor. God does not promise to supply these things though He may well bless ones with some of these. Whatever I need on earth God will supply even to the end of my life and then when that time comes, He will give me courage to face death if God decides to call me home.

Like Moses, I was asking "how Lord" instead of saying "I trust You, Lord." However, God is an understanding and forgiving God as well as a faithful God. What He starts He will finish, and I soon was to learn that God's way is not my way. He who opens the door will furnish the necessary requirements to make it possible for me to enter through that door.

Double Your Talent the Lord's Way

I was taught by my mother to take my need to the Lord and to no other especially if it was a money matter. I never could ask people for money and never will either, so I asked the Lord to show me how I would raise the money. This He did in a most surprising way.

God gives each one of us talents. Some He gives many to, others less, and some even only one talent but everyone is given at least one. I believe very strongly if you do not use your talent given by God, He will take it from you and give it to someone else who will. We see this in the story of the parable of the talents.

> *"For the kingdom of heaven is as a man travelling into a far country, who called his own servants, and delivered unto them his goods. And unto one he gave five talents, to another two, and to another one; to every man according to his several ability; and straightway took his journey. Then he that had received the five talents went and traded with the same, and made them other five talents. And likewise he that had received two, he also gained other two. But he that had received one went and digged in the earth, and hid his lord's money. After a long time the lord of those servants cometh, and reckoneth with them. And so he that had received five talents came and brought other five talents, saying,*

Lord, thou deliveredst unto me five talents: behold, I have gained beside them five talents more. His lord said unto him, Well done, thou good and faithful servant: thou hast been faithful over a few things, I will make thee ruler over many things: enter thou into the joy of thy lord. He also that had received two talents came and said, Lord, thou deliveredst unto me two talents: behold, I have gained two other talents beside them. His lord said unto him, Well done, good and faithful servant; thou hast been faithful over a few things, I will make thee ruler over many things: enter thou into the joy of thy lord. Then he which had received the one talent came and said, Lord, I knew thee that thou art an hard man, reaping where thou hast not sown, and gathering where thou hast not strawed: And I was afraid, and went and hid thy talent in the earth: lo, there thou hast that is thine. His lord answered and said unto him, Thou wicked and slothful servant, thou knewest that I reap where I sowed not, and gather where I have not strawed: Thou oughtest therefore to have put my money to the exchangers, and then at my coming I should have received mine own with usury. Take therefore the talent from him, and give it unto him which hath ten talents. For unto every one that hath shall be given, and he shall have abundance: but from him that hath not shall be taken away even that which he hath." Matthew 25:14-29

Christ tells us before the lord and master went away, he gave a servant five talents, another two talents, and another one talent. When the lord returned each had to give an account of how they used their talents. The servants that used their talents were commended but the one who did not use his talent was reprimanded and the talent taken from him and it given to the servant that used his talents the most. I had to learn this lesson, but it was a great lesson and a great experience for me.

Let me go back in time and lead into this lesson.

I was born outside Moneymore, County Londonderry, in the town land of Ballydawley to parents William George and Mary Elizabeth McCullagh. My father was a farmer. There were four siblings, three girls and one boy, and I was the youngest of the family. My brother, George, was born with severe Down's Syndrome and though he is much older than me he was and is always my little brother and greatly loved.

Our home was a Christian home and Mummy and Daddy loved the Lord. We were brought up to go to Sunday school and Church. My Mother often told me about many children around the world who did not have enough to eat. As you may well understand, with all our food readily available and plentiful I could not fathom why others could and would go hungry.

People who know me know my love for crafts and music. This was instilled in me from as early an age as I can remember. My mother saw the artistic and designing skills in me at an early age and she nurtured and encouraged me to develop these. Before I even started school at four years of age I was knitting and sewing. I was taught early not to waste time as time was one thing I could never redeem. If I was to sit down, I was always given something to do with my hands. I was taught to not only knit and sew but taught both hand and machine sewing, embroidery, crochet, and tapestry. As a result, to this day, I would feel guilty if I were to sit down without having something in my hands to work on. As time and years went past, I added to these crafts and amongst these was to be painting and jewellery making.

I have to confess that God did give me many talents and I really enjoy them, amongst them piano playing and silver making. Initially I thought that my talents were for my own enjoyment, but God had other plans. When the door opened for me to speak around the various churches, I was asked as part of my "presentation" to demonstrate my painting. Having made a promise to God that I would use every opportunity to share with people the Gospel of Jesus Christ I have a prerequisite when being booked; that is that I must be given time to bring the Word of God to the people present.

I am not under any illusion that sometimes the only reason I get an invite to speak is because they want to see and enjoy my painting. Now that is not a problem but that is not my main or primary purpose so when I receive an invitation to speak, I make it clear how I operate. As I demonstrate my painting, I share my testimony and then I do a short reading and bring the Word. I then give the invitation for souls to give their life to Christ and invite anyone to come forward who wishes to be prayed for. This is how I conclude my part of the meeting. That was all I endeavoured to do until people started to ask me if I could bring along painted items for sale. Then when people got to know that I made wedding jewellery they asked me to bring along items of jewellery I had made.

When the trip to Africa came along, I asked the Lord to show me how and where the money was to come from. He quickly answered but not in the way I expected. The Lord did with me as He did with Moses over six thousand years ago. One day not long after praying for guidance to a means of raising money, I was sitting painting when I felt God say to me, "What is that in your hand?" It was my paint brush and I said to the Lord that I did not know what He was telling me. Then it came; "Eileen, let Me have your paintbrush; you paint as much as you can, to the very best of your ability, and leave the rest to Me." Wow! What a revelation from the Lord. It had never even crossed my mind. But why should I not use the talents God had bestowed on me to further the work in His kingdom? This is scriptural after all. I can hear some of you reading this saying that I knew the scripture of the talents so why did I not already think on these things. How often have we all said about certain situations that we could not see the wood for the trees? It was so obvious, yet I could not see it until the Lord actually showed to me.

Immediately I looked for new ideas and inspiration. God blessed me greatly and I soon started to receive orders for painted creamery cans, signs, giftware, and other wooden items. Then I went on to paint glass and the orders kept coming. Alongside this I was alternating between the painting and jewellery making, even designing and making the complete jewellery range for bridal parties. What was God doing? I soon became aware that as I obeyed God, He was creating the openings for my items to be sold and money gathered to meet needs. Some weeks, as I left the travel clinic thanking God for the money to pay the bill that week, I was also asking God for the money to meet the need for the next week. Always God met the need. I could never anticipate how but right on time He always came through for me and met the need. I praise His Holy name yet again as I write this because I know it was God performing miracle after miracle in my life. A lady that I had never met before called at my door with materials for beading and said she wanted me to have them to help with the ministry in Africa. Ladies in a church gifted me pencils, pens, and other items for the children in schools. A chemist gave me medication to take. A lady gave me wee hats that her mother had knit, and other ladies gave me knitted blankets and garments for children.

A great need for pastors in Africa is study materials and study bibles. I have a precious couple who own the coffee shop "Restored" in Ballymoney and they gifted me new bibles which they had purchased for me to take out to pastors. These are always received with great joy and appreciation.

When I shared with the people how God had called me to go to Africa, they would ask me who or what umbrella I was going out under. This caused some raised eyebrows when I replied that I was totally independent and would travel solo in the physical but not alone spiritually because God had promised to go with me. When I sold some products at the meetings or on a one-to-one I held this money separate for Africa. Little did anyone ever guess that the talents God had given me would be the source for much funding for the ministry I was just about to commence.

"What is that in thine hand?" was a statement much before me. I was to see that no matter how small or how weak I thought the thing in my hand was when I gave it to God, it became great. Let me say here again; when your life is owned by God whatever you use for Him becomes His property. In the life of Moses, it was his rod. In the life of Eileen, at this stage in my life, it is my paintbrush and jewellery tools. The rod was just a staff, a walking stick for Moses but when he gave the staff to God a miracle took place and it became God's staff because God had touched it.

Earlier I said that everyone has been given at least one talent and it is incumbent of each one of us to know what it is and then to utilise that talent for the glory of God. People have said to me that it is easy for me as I am multi-talented. That is as maybe but the more given to me by God the more is expected from God, so the more accountable I am to God. This I must remember.

Many times, we are so focused on the need we forget the important part — the journey. We're asking God or desiring to have our own home, a car, a new suit, or a holiday and each one of those can be an end goal. However, we may not have the money to attain one of them. The devil highlights what we don't have causing us to focus on the end goal, that which we don't have while all the time God is saying, "What is in your hand?"

The Word of God says in Zechariah 4:10, *"For who hath despised the day of small things?"*

This was something I was to prove over and over. My mother frequently told us, "Take care of the pennies and the pounds will take care of themselves." In other words, if I look after the little I have it will soon accumulate into a bigger quantity. The scripture above is saying, though the instruments are weak and unlikely, yet God often chooses such, to bring about great things by them. It is not right to despise a small beginning because given time it can become something great.

God focuses on the small seed you and I offer up to Him now at this moment in time and we need to allow tomorrow to look after itself. How often I am guilty of thinking and talking about what I do not have. I say that I have not the money to buy land for a church in Uganda or such like. Instead I should be focusing on what I do have and to thank God for His blessings bestowed on me. God has made a way for me to have money in 'God's ministry' box to send to a pastor requiring provision for rent or for the work in his church. This was never more apparent than when the need arose for a church to be established in a village. I was well aware of the need and Pastor Godfrey Mugolo and I were praying for God's guidance. It became clear that we needed to buy the land and then build the church. The problem then arose to who was going to sell us some land? If the land ever became available what would be the cost and where would the money come from? We prayed much for God to open the way to obtain a plot and in the meantime, I saved any funds that came my way. Pound coins were put in a small container and two-pound coins into another wee container. Spare change became a prisoner for God's ministry. It was not long until I saw the few pounds that were thrown into the container add up to substantial amounts.

Then the test came. An emergency arose where money was required for a brother in the Lord in Uganda. What was I to do? My storehouse was being filled for a major project — the purchase of land and the building of a church, I could not afford to take what was saved and use it for something else, even though it was still in the field of ministry. As I prayed, I sensed strongly that I should meet this urgent need and trust God for everything else. The next day, with the love of God in my heart to bless the pastor in great need, I sent the money through. In the interim I was painting and making jewellery to sell around the meetings which I was speaking at. Also, people would ask for items I had made, and the money received would go into the savings for Africa. Sometimes it would only be £2 or £3 pounds, sometimes £20 or £30, and yet other times more. Each amount small or great was a step closer to the end goal and a cause for celebration. Each pound saved today, tomorrow, and the next day was so great and before long I was realising I was moving along the long journey to my goal. How I would praise God for His faithfulness to me.

One day I received word that land was up for sale and it was very suitable for the church. I was excited and asked the Pastors to pray and then view it and ascertain the price. I and my prayer partners here were also in prayer. The report came back that it was perfect, and we knew the figure we needed to raise to purchase it. We all got down to prayer and made our petitions known to the Lord.

Approximately two months passed. One day a couple came to see me and what I was told was totally amazing. They were aware of the great need for land and a church built on it. They had money they were gifting to the Lord and after prayer they felt led by God to gift it to God's ministry in Africa that I was involved in. When they handed me a sealed envelope, they said they trusted it was enough to buy the land and build the church. Later when I opened it imagine my surprise to find a very large cheque enclosed inside. Tears flowed down my cheeks as I praised and thanked God for answered prayer and for the love and sacrifice of this dear couple.

Why have I shared this with you? I want you to see how if we are faithful and obedient to God and give what we have to Him in faith today, small though it may be in our eyes, God will take care of our need in the 'tomorrow' no matter how large it may seem to us. Matthew 6:34; *"Take therefore no thought for the morrow: for the morrow shall take thought for the things of itself."* also comes to mind here. I serve an awesome and majestic God and it always humbles me when I think how He has chosen someone like me to be part of His work internationally. He has given me the talents of painting and jewellery making to be used to help spread the good news of the gospel across the world.

But what is your talent? What has God given you and are you using it for God, and using it to the full? Are you saying you have no idea what your talent is? If that is the case, then go before God and ask Him to show you the talent or talents He has given you. I find other people can often indicate to me where my talents lie. This was evident when it came to teaching as I did not think I was a good teacher until people kept telling me I was. God forbid that this should come across to you as prideful, not at all, but rather to indicate sometimes God uses others to highlight to us things we are good at.

What sort of things might be given as a talent? Let me look at this from a Christian or a church angle and see how, if given to God, it can be the very hand of God itself.

- The ability to work among the children. Christ gave the command to Peter to feed the lambs first before He gave the commandment to feed the sheep. (John 21:15-17)
- A willing heart to share your testimony wherever you find yourself. In the workplace, in the community, with neighbours, in mother and toddlers, in the classroom. You become a voice for God.
- Open up your home to hospitality. If you can cook or bake use this skill for the Lord. Share a meal with someone in need or with someone who would benefit from a little show of love.
- Do coffee mornings when you can invite people in to share in bible study. If you have a spare room offer it to a missionary who is visiting local churches, a preacher or someone who is in need of a wee break. Something my husband and I have is an open house policy where people are always welcome to come for a chat or for prayer and the kettle is on the boil.
- Can you play an instrument? Play it to the glory of God
- Are you good with small children? Then offer your services in children's work.
- An important talent is being able to visit the elderly in their home or in the nursing home and read the scriptures, pray and take time for a wee chat.
- Perhaps you are a good listener and slow to speak. Someone can tell you their fears and you can give good counsel because you have started your day with God, and He guides you.

Whatever God has blessed you with give it to God and allow God to use it to His Glory. It will amaze you what God will do. The blessings you enjoy in return are immeasurable.

The things in my hand that God was using were to help fund the ministry in Africa. There were bibles required, school rooms needing to be built, items required for prisoners such as soap, pencils, pens, books, clothes for children, and items needed for pastors and their church such as building materials equipment and money to buy food for children. However, God was to take me to another level.

The year was 2016 and after a few visits to Uganda and Kenya God showed me that the poverty was rampant through the land. The two priorities for the people were food to exist and money to pay school fees to enable the children to attend school. No money for fees, then the children would go uneducated. I came across children who never made it through primary school. This I found heart-breaking so again I asked God what I could do. There were sponsors for just a few children, but it was only a drop in the ocean.

There is an old proverb that I hold strongly to and it is: "Give a man a fish and you feed him a day. Teach a man to fish and you feed him for life."

The Lord again asked me what was in my hand and again it was my paintbrush and jewellery tools. That was when the Lord gave me the idea of teaching the people a skill. Then this skill could be used to earn money or exchange for food.

With this in mind I spoke to our main contact in Kenya, Pastor Antony Shimenga in Kagamega, who thought it was a good idea and chose to plan something further. Pastor

Godfrey Mugolo put together a schedule for Uganda. Both men arranged the place and the people who were to attend, and I would give a few days in each place to teaching painting. I was also to take a select few people and teach them jewellery making. These people would be in a position of leadership and would in turn teach others.

What had I let myself into? How was I going to fund this? I knew I could not do it on my own so again I brought the need to the Lord. One night I woke in the middle of the night with the clear thought of contacting my paint supplier who I did teaching and demonstrating for. Would they be prepared to help me seemed a tall ask but ask I would. Again, I asked the Lord to go before me and prepare their hearts which He did, and a company agreed to supply the products for the two countries. Not only did they supply the paints, but they forwarded them to my two pastors who were arranging everything in their country. Absolutely everything that was needed for all the participants, except for the brushes, the company supplied. Some people gave me money and I was able to put enough money together to buy a full range of brushes for everyone.

The numbers attending the classes were large in Uganda, but the people were very keen to learn. The composition of those attending was both young men and women in their teens right through to community leaders and mature men and woman. Not only did the ages vary but also their religious background. There were Muslims, Seven Day Adventists, Catholics, and those saved into the family of God all together learning to paint and also make jewellery. Through this I was also able to share my love for the Lord and the Lord's love for each one of them. This was my reason to be in their nations sharing the gospel first and foremost and then my talents which the Lord had blessed me with.

When it came to sunset the people would keep working on at their painting project with only the light of a phone to illuminate their work. There was one young man in particular and he was a born artist and never knew because it was the first time he had held a paintbrush or worked with paints. I confess I was very proud of him. Another young man that amazed me was my Ugandan son, Pastor Godfrey. Besides still interpreting for me he was very keen to learn to paint. We all had many laughs because he was so caught up with his painting that he would forget to interpret something I had just said. I said that in the west the ladies always said men could not multi-task, they could only do one thing at a time, and so we teased Pastor Godfrey continually, especially when a young lady attending, who was a teacher, would have to interpret for the few who had missed out. This young man, Pastor Godfrey Mugolo, was a natural both at painting and jewellery making. Everything he was shown and taught he was able to learn and apply it immediately. When we moved from Uganda to Kenya, he was so good he was able to assist me in the teaching. Pastor Godfrey has gone on to sell much of what he makes, and I am proud to say he is very professional now and can share his skills with others in turn. This is what God expects of you and me. We are to use our talents to bless others who in turn can follow through and bless other people also. It is just like a domino effect, once the movement starts it continues on through.

After finishing in Uganda Pastor Godfrey and I travelled on to Rwanda and after ministering in some churches there we then travelled on to Niarobi Kenya. Pastor Godfrey and I had left Rwanda early in the morning to travel to Niarobi in the East of Kenya and then a further long bus journey to Kakamega in the Northwest of the country. We arrived eventually the next morning at eight o'clock, with Pastor Antony Shimenga, in the village of Handidi, a short distance from the town of Kakamega.

The paints had arrived, and Pastor Antony had a big marquee, loaned to him, erected at his home. That first night, late after we were all settled down in bed for the night visitors arrived. It was an Archbishop and a Bishop from Tanzania. They had heard reports of my teaching and preaching so had travelled to "check me out" before extending an invitation to me to teach and preach in Tanzania. It was 'close fellowship' in the small home with the two visitors and Pastor Godfrey sharing one room and me sharing with a lady who had also travelled to learn to paint. The fellowship was great though I could not speak Swahili and the Arch Bishop did not understand me. My accent was one problem but coming from Northern Ireland, United Kingdom, I tend to speak a little too fast. The Bishop did the interpreting between me and the Archbishop. Suffice to say we laughed much especially every time anyone said "Kakamega" Pastor Antony explained what 'Kakamega' stood for and as he explained he did the actions. Let me share this with you here please.

It was when the colonists were eating 'Ugali' which to you and me in the west is maize, as they were pulling of a handful of ugali the natives would say 'Khakhameka'. The whites did not quite catch the Swahili pronunciation and to them it sounded as Kakamega. So the name was given to the county and so it has remained and the county called to this day.

The Arch Bishop would start to laugh, and he had such an infectious laugh he had us all immediately laughing uncontrollably. Even to this day mention the place 'Kakamega' to him and it still cause him great laughter.

The people I was to teach painting to were known as *"Beyond 2030 Community Group"* at Handidi village of Shinyalu the sub County of Kakamega County. You can imagine my shock when I went out to set up and as the people gathered, they numbered thirty-four. Along with the Bishops present other pastors came along and attended. Pastors Samuel Arogo, Richard Masika, Edward Asembo, and other people came along to observe and to also have fellowship with one another.

Each day the people worked hard, and we put in long hours. It was such a thrill to see the people eager to learn painting but more so for me was the opportunity to witness to many people. We commenced each morning with devotions, and we fellowshipped when we took a short break. The gospel was shared, and invitations given to the people to attend the crusade and meetings.

Praise God I did indeed see some of these in the meetings, but above all I saw souls saved at both crusades and churches. This was and is the main purpose of God's ministry which I am privileged to serve in. This is what I must keep focused upon. I never knew, when sitting at the knee of my mother, that one day my skills being learned early in life God would hone and use to open doors for people to hear the Gospel of Jesus Christ. But why should I be surprised when God used a shepherd's staff carried by Moses to perform wondrous miracles for the Children of Israel?

My question to you is: What has God put in *your* hand? Do you wonder how God might use you? See what He has given you. God equips people in various ways. I like to have people over to my home, you might say. Another might respond "I'm good with my hands," "I can help a group get things done," "I like to cook," "I have the gift of working with children," "I like to keep things tidy," and so on.

Offer to God in faith what He has given you, no matter how simple, and God will use it — sometimes supernaturally

— to do His work. You'll have a new sense of meaning, since you'll begin to realize how God is using simple things in new and wonderful ways. When I reflect on my own life it never ceases to amaze me How God has worked down over the years. Even when I was complacent God still never let me go.

A Boy's Picnic Meets the Need of the Hour

We read in Mathew 9:10-17 of the miracle Christ performed when He fed the five thousand. When Jesus saw a hungry crowd, he said to his disciples: "You feed them." They were stunned by the magnitude of the need. So, Jesus brought it down to their level. "Okay, Andrew, do a little inventory. Find out what food we have on hand." Andrew checked around. "There's a boy here with five loaves (wee scones) and two fishes. So what good is that amongst so many?" Jesus ignored his unbelief. He took the bread and the fish, lifted them to God in thanksgiving, and then began to distribute them to the people until all 5,000 plus women and children had been fed.

That's how God's work gets done. By weak people doing an inventory, and then offering to Jesus what they find.

God has a world to save. You're just one person. What difference can you make? I encourage you to do this simple inventory — count your blessings, see what God has given you. That way, when God asks you, "What's that in your hand?" you won't answer: "Nothing! I have nothing." You'll be able to tell Him — and then you can let Him use the gift / skill / resource / interest / relationship / opportunity to His glory.

Once more, what is in *your* hand?

If you have a tendency to despair over lost opportunities or if you worry about the future, ask yourself this question: "What is right in front of me?" In other words, what circumstances and relationships are currently available to you? This question can get your focus off a past regret or a scary future and back to what God can do in your life.

It's similar to the question God asked Moses at the burning bush. Moses was troubled. Aware of his own weaknesses, he expressed fear about the Lord's call for him to lead Israel out of bondage. So God simply asked Moses, *"What is that in your hand?"* (Exodus 4:2). The Lord shifted Moses' attention away from his anxiety about the future and suggested he notice what was right in front of him — a shepherd's rod. God showed Moses that He could use this ordinary staff to perform miracles as a sign for unbelieving people. As Moses' trust in God grew, so did the magnitude of miracles God worked through His servant.

Do you think about past failures too much? Do you have fearful thoughts about the future? Recall God's question: *"What is that in your hand?"* What current circumstances and relationships can God use for your benefit and His glory? Entrust them — and your life — to Him. He will not fail you.

If God can use a shepherd's staff; if God can use a paintbrush and paints; if God can use a needle and thread; if God can use jewellery tools to expand His kingdom, God can use whatever is in your hand. All you have to do is give it totally and freely to the Lord and God will do the rest.

Out-of-Body Experience

Have you ever wondered about death? I know I have thought about death often and what experience I would go through if I were to die. Would it be a painful experience? Would it be a frightening experience? Would I suffer great distress as my heart stopped beating and my lungs ceased taking in oxygen? I had witnessed people tell loved ones not to weep. They were not afraid to die as they knew they were going to be with their Saviour. How come they had absolutely no fear? Secretly I was harbouring a fear of death and I could not tell anyone.

The year was 1978 and the day was Saturday, 25th February. It started as any other day with me enjoying my breakfast, but it was short lived, and little did anyone realise what the day ahead was to hold.

I had been admitted to hospital a week earlier in labour with my second child. The problem was that the baby was not due for another ten weeks. Throughout the pregnancy sickness was never far away and generally it was not an easy time. When I was admitted the Senior Registrar decided that they would stop labour and hopefully I would carry the baby to the due date. The other problem was that the baby was very small for thirty weeks and they wanted to give it a chance of survival. It was an experience I would never wish to go through ever again as the pain was excruciating but they succeeded in stopping labour and I was kept lying throughout the following week. I was feeling very weak and exhausted, so I tended to sleep much of the day and night. On the morning in question the nurse said I could be pillowed up to eat breakfast. I was in a single room and as I was eating breakfast the nurse was writing up my notes. It was almost immediately that I felt the first pains and realised I had started labour again. It was all action from the medical team yet again. The doctor came and sat on the bed beside me. As he held my hand, he tried to reassure me the team would take really good care of me.

The doctor advised me labour would have to be allowed to take its course and they would look after me and make things as easy as possible, but the baby could not survive. We discussed all the pros and cons, but they all agreed the baby was much too small to live. Off I went, was wired up to various machines, and time progressed. I thought labour would be very easy because the baby was so small, but this was not to be the case. It was long and severe. I remember clearly the baby crying when it was born and I begging the doctor to not let my baby, a boy, die. He quickly told me it could not survive many minutes as he was even smaller than they expected.

Just then I felt something peculiar happening to me and I went to speak and ask for help, but I could not speak. I quickly thought I would reach out and catch one of the team to alert them that I needed urgent help. I was in distress, but I could not move my arm. I tried to move my leg but nothing. I was starting to panic as I knew something serious was going wrong and nobody seemed to be aware. However, in those few seconds, which to me were several minutes, the machine started to bleep and quickly a nurse put an oxygen mask over my mouth and nose. By now I could not breathe at all, but I felt the cool air entering my lungs with no effort from me. What on earth was happening to me?

The next thing I realised I was leaving my body and was up in the far corner of the room watching back at my body. Despite the fact I was looking at what was happening I became aware I was travelling to a tremendous sunshine or bright light that was behind me. The team hit the crash button and the crash team came running in and started to work on my body. I watched it all from where I was suspended and listened to everything they said and I thought, "they think I am in that 'wardrobe' of a body, but I am not there. I am gone and I do not want to go back there again." The pain I had been in was all gone, worry and stress of the situation were no more, and I was enveloped in a great calm that no words could ever describe. To be honest, I had no thought for the baby boy just born or for family I had left behind. I was in perfect assurance that I was going to Jesus and these 'stupid professionals' did not realise I did not want to go back. I was 'out of it'! I was dead!

The team put in lines and then they were taking me to theatre as fast as possible to see if they could save my life. As they discussed this, I was laughing to myself thinking they were the ones needing help *not* me. A nurse asked about ringing my husband to come as quickly as possible but was told there was no time; everyone was needed. I heard and saw everything that was said and done and while you might think it would have scared me, the opposite was the case. They dismounted machines from the stands put them on the bed and started out the room and down the long corridor to theatre running as fast as they could while pushing the bed with the body on it. I remember, again smiling to myself and saying, "they think I am in that body, but they do not know there is nothing there. I am back here very fine indeed. What a waste of time and effort. Do they not know?"

As they were running with the bed to reach theatre, I followed behind at a distance observing all, but the bright light of sunshine was also at my back. Even though I heard everything and saw everything I felt nothing but joy, peace, and total calmness. Friend, I cannot stress enough the total feeling of utter bliss and peace I was in and even when they were working on the body, putting in lines, it was as if they were working on a wardrobe that had housed me but I was long departed and it was just an empty carcase now.

When in theatre I must have gone back into an unconscious state again for it was a couple of days later when I awoke in my room with a nurse at my side. She called the doctor. He was gentle but I knew he was relieved to see me able to speak. I told him what had happened to me and he asked me to stop as he wanted to bring in some staff. Shortly he returned with all the staff that was present at the time of the trauma. He asked me to recount all the detail of my experience. I saw the shock register on some of the faces and when I was finished, he addressed the team and me.

Effectively they had lost me. I had 'flat lined' in medical terms. I had died for a few minutes and it was only when they got me to theatre and operated that they were able to resuscitate me, and I went into a coma for a time. The Senior Registrar explained to the junior staff that is why they are told in training to be careful how they speak around an unconscious or dying patient. The hearing is the last thing to leave the body and though they may think the patient has passed away the patient will still hear what is being said. He then told us all that what I had experienced was an "out-of-body experience." They were astounded that I was able to describe in detail every single thing said and done. The team knew, too, in the natural that I could not have possibly known equipment that was used on me when I was 'dead'. It was the source of many discussions with the staff and my visitors in the days that followed. My consultant asked me how I felt now after knowing what had happened and was I scared? To this I could give a resounding "no!"

During this time things were difficult for my husband. He received the phone call to come immediately to the hospital. When he arrived, he was taken to the office and the team told him I was still fighting for life. The baby was alive - just - and he should have it christened immediately. Poor Ian did not know what to do or where to turn. He had a wife that was holding on to life by a thread and a baby that would die at any moment. Ian went straight to the minister and Ian's father was already there. The minister went quickly to the hospital and saw us both and returned to the manse where his wife had made tea for Ian and his father. The minister said he had prayed over the two of us and he refused to baptise the baby as the baby would live and we would bring the baby to the church and present him to the Lord when the time was right. That is exactly what happened. It was a rollercoaster of emotions as one day the baby was holding and feeding and the next day, he was very unwell again. I was home from hospital but in every day to spend time with my "wee man" Derek. I promised the Lord if He would allow Derek to survive, I would present him back to the Lord. Eventually Derek weighed the 'magical' five and a half pounds and was discharged from hospital. It was with great joy we presented him to the Lord on Sunday, 14th May 1978 - my birthday.

Perhaps you are reading this and would wish to ask me why I am so emphatic with my answer. Let me answer the question this way, please. I had always had a fear of death and dying. Put another way, nobody I knew had come back to share their experience of the death angel coming. Because I was a child of God, I felt I could not tell anyone of my fears as this would be so wrong — even sinful to admit I was afraid to die. It was that passage from life in the body here to being face to face with Christ my Saviour I feared so much. So, I asked God to show me what death was like to ease my mind and alleviate my fears. Be careful what you ask God for as He can take you at your word. I never thought God would literally allow me to taste of death, but He did. Not what I would have chosen but it has taught me so much. Be careful what you ask for!

I have proved that we are a tripartite being made up of body, soul, and spirit. The body was created by God from dust and to dust it shall return. But God breathed into man and man became a living soul. My soul belongs to God and as a child of God saved by the precious Blood of Christ; my soul goes to be with Christ. My soul and your soul never dies, and there are only two destinations: heaven or hell. The spirit of man worships and as a child of God I worship Christ. When you die and when I die our soul and spirit lives on outside of the body.

For me, it proved the moment my last breath leaves my body I am free. No longer captive in the body like clothes in a wardrobe but released and travelling to be with Christ. Before a family member can even have time to notify an undertaker about my death the upper-taker has me out of there. Released from pain, sorrow, sickness, anxiety, longings, fear, lacking in this world, and no more crying. It is true:

There'll be no sorrow there,
No more burdens to bear,
No more sickness, no pain,
No more parting over there;
And forever I will be,
With the One who died for me,
What a day, glorious day that will be.

What a day that will be,
When my Jesus I shall see,
And I look upon His face,
The One who saved me by His grace;
When He takes me by the hand,
And leads me through the Promised Land,
What a day, glorious day that will be.
(copyright Jim Hill)

It was through this I destroyed the belief of some people in soul sleep. What a lie. It truly is "absent from the body and present with the Lord."

When my godly mother passed away, I remember being devastated at losing my mother when I was still so very young — 25 years of age — but looking around the bedroom and telling her how much I loved her. I knew she was away to be with Christ which, for her, was far better. Death is nothing to fear for the child of God. It is the last enemy and Christ has already conquered death, hell, and the grave for us. Hallelujah. What a Saviour.

If you do not know this Jesus Christ of whom I talk about you can know Him now. All you have to do is to:

1. Admit you are a sinner
2. Believe Jesus Christ is the Son of God and Saviour of the world
3. Confess your need of Salvation and cleansing in Christ's Blood
4. Decide to live for Him every day of your life
5. Explain the gospel to others through sharing your testimony of God's saving and keeping power in your life.

It is as easy as A, B, C, D, E. If you do this, you are now 'saved'.

May this help everyone who reads my experience today to understand more about death? If you are truly saved you too, like me, can face death without fear knowing it is nothing as Christ is with you. Even more, it is a beautiful experience for the child of God.

"Be ye ready for ye no not what a day may bring forth."

My little son, against all odds, survived and has blessed us beyond all measure. Such love he showers on me no mother could ask for more. It was not easy for the first few weeks but one day at a time. People were praying for this little miracle who weighed in at two pounds, three ounces and nine weeks early. But God had a plan for His life and a purpose Derek was to fulfil. God overruled and proved He is the Great Physician and what satan had planned to destroy and kill God said "No! He shall not die but live. What a mighty God we serve. "I thank you Lord for my beautiful son." Derek is now a man of 40 years of age. God spared the life of my precious son and God spared my life also. There was a work and a plan for both lives.

I started this chapter in my life with questions to God, but God closed this chapter in my life having given me all the answers. The Lord's ways are not our ways, but the Lord's ways are always the best ways.

Love, Marriage and Eternal Love

"Beloved, let us love one another: for love is of God; and every one that loveth is born of God, and knoweth God. He that loveth not knoweth not God; for God is love. In this was manifested the love of God toward us, because that God sent his only begotten Son into the world, that we might live through him. Herein is love, not that we loved God, but that he loved us, and sent his Son to be the propitiation for our sins. Beloved, if God so loved us, we ought also to love one another. No man hath seen God at any time. If we love one another, God dwelleth in us, and his love is perfected in us. Hereby know we that we dwell in him, and he in us, because he hath given us of his Spirit. And we have seen and do testify that the Father sent the Son to be the Saviour of the world. Whosoever shall confess that Jesus is the Son of God, God dwelleth in him, and he in God. And we have known and believed the love that God hath to us. God is love; and he that dwelleth in love dwelleth in God, and God in him. Herein is our love made perfect, that we may have boldness in the day of judgment: because as he is, so are we in this world. There is no fear in love; but perfect love casteth out fear: because fear hath torment. He that feareth is not made perfect in love. We love him, because he first loved us. If a man say, I love God, and hateth his brother, he is a liar: for he that loveth not his brother whom he hath seen, how can he love God

whom he hath not seen? And this commandment have we from him, That he who loveth God love his brother also." 1John 4:7-21

Every girl dreams of getting married and I was no different. My oldest sister, Elizabeth, was married quite a few years earlier and I had lived through all the planning and excitement for months beforehand. There were bridal magazines lying about and I would spend hours gazing through the pages filled with beautiful brides in all their finery, looking like regal princesses. Many of the gowns were heavily embroidered white dresses with long trains, the white representing purity. There were glittering headdresses that were like royal crowns, and spectacular jewellery chosen carefully and worn to complement the dresses. Hairstyles and make-up were done to perfection and then the floral boutiques that were carried, spoke of the beauty of nature and the love the young lady has for her bridegroom. Tradition dictates that the bride's sisters or close friends would be invited to attend the bride on her big day and they too would be beautifully attired in such a fashion as to compliment the bride but to not outshine her on this momentous day in her life.

The bride-to-be would have been saving diligently for many years for her big day; the most important and greatly longed for event in her life. She would want to have the very best of everything her savings could afford. Everything would be carefully planned right down to the very last and minute detail. She would want to look her very best for her darling bridegroom.

The bridegroom would equally have been preparing for the day he would take to himself a wife to love and to cherish. On that morning he, too, would be dressed in all his finery accompanied by his best man and groomsman. He would have made sure his bride would arrive at the church in style with the transport having been booked months ahead. But more importantly he would have secured a home in which he and his wife could start of their married life together after returning from their honeymoon – a special holiday that he would have planned for themselves following the wedding day. The invitations would have been sent out at least six weeks before the date and guest would be busy planning their wedding garments also. When the day would arrive it would be a very early start for the bride and the groom and during the solemn ceremony in the church in front of all their guests the couple would make their vows to each other and before God, to love, honour and obey, for richer or poorer, in sickness and in health till death they do part. Then after the ceremony in the church the celebrations would begin.

My sister's wedding followed this pattern and my sister, Dorothy, and I were her bridesmaids. This was like a window into what I could expect when my time would come as come it did. But let me go back and tell you about how my husband and I met.

I was in my early teens at the Rainey Endowed School in Magherafelt when the word was spread that a big Gospel Crusade was planned for Magherafelt. The preacher was to be Evangelist Mr. Hedley Murphy and his brother, Mr. James Murphy, was going to train a great choir that would lead the praise and worship. Choir practices were to commence immediately after Christmas, and I was invited to join the choir. I have always loved music so there was no encouragement required however I would have to ask my parents and if I was permitted my daddy would be needed to drive me to each practice. There was not a problem and my parents granted my request. I never missed a meeting of the choir. When July of the same year came a large thousand-seater marquee was erected in a field belonging to Mr Samuel James Scott, a local businessman, and the crusade commenced. It was a very hot and dry spell and our uniform proved very suitable. The gentlemen wore grey trousers, white shirts, and a blue tie. The young ladies wore grey skirts and white blouses.

The crowds came flocking in on the first evening and as the ushers seated the congregation it became evident the large marquee was not adequate so after about three day it was extended by a further five hundred seats. Among the ushers I noticed a young man smartly dressed in dark trousers, white shirt and tie, and black blazer. There was something more about this young man, he was very handsome and had lovely blond wavy hair which was neatly groomed. I was captivated by his bright countenance and smile and wondered in my mind who he was and.... was he unattached. I did not think for one moment that he even had seen me at any time but for me the crusade had become even more "interesting". The preaching was powerful and every night there was a great move of the Holy Spirit and souls were saved.

Besides the choir singing in four-part harmony there was also a gentleman, Mr. Tom Laverty from Ballymena, who sang solo, with the choir supporting on the chorus. One piece became a firm favourite of the great assembly of people and Tom would be called on every night to sing it yet again. It had a lasting impression on me also and to this day it is one of my favourite pieces. The words are anointed and meaningful for my daily walk in the Lord. When trials come, I bring these words to remembrance and they encourage me to keep going on.

My heart can sing when I pause to remember
A heartache here is but a stepping stone
Along a trail that's winding always upward,
This troubled world is not my final home.

Chorus
But until then my heart will go on singing,
Until then with joy I'll carry on,
Until the day my eyes behold the city,
Until the day God calls me home.

The things of earth will dim and lose their value
If we recall they're borrowed for awhile;
And things of earth that cause the heart to tremble,
Remembered there will only bring a smile.

This weary world with all its toil and struggle
May take its toll of misery and strife;
The soul of man is like a waiting eagle;
When it's released, it's destined for the skies.

Chorus
But until then my heart will go on singing,
Until then with joy I'll carry on,
Until the day my eyes behold the city,
Until the day God calls me home.

The crusade ended and life returned to normal again. One evening a few months later the doorbell rang, and my sister came back in to tell me there was a young man asking to see me. Surprised because I was not expecting anyone I went to see. The young man asking for me was none other than the young man who I had noted with interest at the crusade. Ian had asked around at the crusade if someone could tell him who I was and where I was from. It was to be a number of months later before he plucked up enough courage to come to my home. I did go out with him, but we decided to remain friends since I was still very young.

Love Shared is a Special Love

Love shared is indeed very special. The friendship that started changed. Love was the gentle stranger that moved in silently and then caught fire. It was so beautiful.

By the time two years had passed my parents had moved to a retirement bungalow mid-way between Ballymena and Antrim. Ian and I started to date seriously and another two years later we married on September 12th 1972. Now, when I speak around church meetings and am sharing my testimony, I always jokingly say I never noticed Ian at the crusade, and it was Ian who came running after me asking me to marry him. However, I can say that from the first moment I saw him there was a connection there and when we did start to date it was mutual love and respect for each other. Ian loved the Lord as did I and we prayed together. It is with praise honour and glory to God alone that I can say with Christ's love in us we in turn loved each other and we never had a cross word the whole time we went out together up to our wedding day.

Our wedding, like my sister's, was planned with meticulous precision. We were married in Ballymena Free Presbyterian Church by Rev. James Beggs. A pastor and preacher I hold in high esteem to this day. Our wedding was all I have desired and more. I was married in a white gown with a long flowing train and carried red roses for my bouquet. My two sisters were bridesmaids and as Ian is an only child his two friends, who were both Faith Mission Pilgrims at the time, Mr. Lloyd Watson and Rev. Hugh Ross, was best man and groomsman.

It was a great day with family and friends gathered in as our wedding guests and my father walked me up the aisle to 'give me away' to my husband. It is tradition here in the United Kingdom that a bride has one very special person take part in her wedding. I was no different as I had someone very special in my life whom I wanted to have a special place and duty to perform that day. It was my brother George, who has severe Downs Syndrome. To George's delight he was all dressed up for the day and he presented me with a silver horseshoe outside on the steps of the church after the ceremony. Even as I pen this it brings tears to my eyes as I recall his joy at being part of my big day and my heart bursting with pride at having him there with the bridal party. As it turns out my wedding was to be the only wedding George was ever to attend.

The Institution of Marriage.

This is what God constituted marriage for. We read in Genesis 2:18 *"And the LORD God said, It is not good that the man should be alone; I will make him an help meet for him."*

> In Genesis 2:21-24, it reads; *"And the LORD God caused a deep sleep to fall upon Adam, and he slept: and he took one of his ribs, and closed up the flesh instead thereof; And the rib, which the LORD God had taken from man, made he a woman, and brought her unto the man. And Adam said, This is now bone of my bones, and flesh of my flesh: she shall be called Woman, because she was taken out of Man. Therefore shall a man leave his father and his mother, and shall cleave unto his wife: and they shall be one flesh."*

> Compare Matthew 19:4-6; *"And he (being Jesus) answered and said unto them, Have ye not read, that he which made them at the beginning made them male*

and female, And said, For this cause shall a man leave father and mother, and shall cleave to his wife: and they twain shall be one flesh? Wherefore they are no more twain, but one flesh. What therefore God hath joined together, let not man put asunder."

The first thing we will notice in Genesis is that although Adam was given charge of all God's great creation and asked to name the creatures, God recognised that Adam was lonely. He had a need for company on a par with himself. Animals, though lovely, could not alleviate the loneliness in the beautiful world. I see that God created man and woman as a way to meet real human needs.

God said in verse 18, "*It is not good that the man should be alone.*" He could have added that it is not good for the woman to be alone either. I know that without Ian I would be very lonely. Recognising man and woman's need God created woman and man together as a beautiful way to meet human needs. He created the marriage relationship as a lifelong relationship with one person. Marriage was always meant to be between one man and one woman. No arguments and no debates! The bible says it and God's Word is final! Marriage between two men or two women is an abomination unto a pure and Holy God.

God's creative work was not fully complete until He made woman. He did not, as He did with Adam, make her from the dust of the ground but chose to make her from man's flesh and bone. In doing this he was emphasising that in marriage man and woman become one flesh. It is a beautiful mystical union of a couple's hearts and lives. It is worth me stating here that throughout the Bible God treats this union very seriously. Adam realised that there was a significant connection to Eve beyond proximity. They both shared DNA. She was literally bone of his bone. They shared God's image. God intended that this meaningful connection would not only address Adam's loneliness but would illustrate the possibility of significant connection to God through Jesus Christ. The connecting word "therefore" links to the concept of oneness and meaningful connection. Because of this God-designed biological and spiritual connection between male and female, God established from the outset the basic foundation for unity in marriage. Why I believe this was intended to be a universal principle is because it was originally presented to Adam and Eve who had no father and mother to leave. It applies to every marriage. Unity in marriage involves three stages. Leaving, Cleaving, and Weaving. I will come back to these three stages later.

Because of the seriousness of marriage my minister, Rev. Beggs, met with me before my marriage to Ian. He wanted to know and ensure that we fully understood and were willing to keep this commitment that would make Ian and I one. Our goal in marriage had to be more than friendship - it had to be oneness.

My father and mother also counselled me before Ian and I became betrothed. They wished to make sure I understood what the scriptures taught regarding marriage and when I left home that day and took my marriage vows before God it was for life. At the first disagreement I could not run back home and expect them to take me back into the family. How I thank God for my parents firm teaching.

I am very well aware that not all marriages are happy and nonviolent. Not in every marriage is the husband or wife faithful to each other. Perhaps the dear wife is striving to rear her wee family on the meagre amount of money gleaned from the alcoholic husband. I am not advocating that the wife be a doormat for a proud dictatorial man either. Not at all! I will go on to put on record here that I believe while an abused wife is bad – nay – disgraceful and sinful, an abused husband is even worse. Sad to say there are many abused men that have either come through or are in this situation. I have met young men who have been driven almost to suicide by a cruel, uncaring, and unloving wife. Those girls will be called to give an account before God.

Age has no bearing on what constitutes a good marriage. I was just seventeen when I married, and Ian was only twenty-one. Many said our marriage would never last and some gave us just one year. We proved them wrong praise God. How come our marriage was different from many of our friends who married? We had Christ in our marriage, and He was the unseen guest in our home. Christ makes the difference! His love for us knows no bounds. Christ is everything to me.

Our love was and is a love that understands each other and shares everything. It is a love that would and does forgive through good times and bad times. It does not seek its own way but allows for human frailties. This we practice to this present day, though we do not always get things right we ask forgiveness of each other and it is forgotten. A few nights before our wedding we pledged to each other that we would put the phrase from scripture found in Ephesian 4:26 into action in our marriage from day one; *"Let not the sun go down upon your wrath."*

This simply put means any arguments or disagreements (and there would be many throughout life) would either be settled, or we would agree to differ, but we would not take the argument to bed with us and rise with it the next day. It was forgotten by bedtime – end of story period! This decision implemented has proved a stalwart in our marriage.

I believe strongly, and proved it in my own life, that when a woman has the love of a good man, a family and circle of loyal friends she is rich. Though she were to gain the whole world it would never be enough to satisfy. Money cannot purchase life, liberty or love. This love can never be expressed but can only be spelled out in heart-to-heart living from "this day forward till death us do part." I am hoping all things for the future and I choose to forget all things that are past. That is how I choose to live my married life as wife with and to my husband. I am nothing in everyday life without Ian and I love him with all my heart but my first love hast to be Jesus Christ my Saviour.

As you read this you may smile even laugh at some of the things I have shared in Ian and my days of courtship, but I want you to read this and learn from our story. Why? Christ's relationship to all the men and woman, boys and girls who have put their trust in Him is also compared to a bride prepared for her husband, a spiritual marriage to come. These people, including me are His Church, the Bride of Christ and He is our Bridegroom. I will go into this deeper in a moment.

God gave marriage as a gift to Adam and Eve. They were created perfect for each other. Marriage was not just for convenience nor was it to please any traditions but brought about by God and has three basic actions and aspects. I mentioned them briefly earlier in the chapter. These are:

1. **Leaving:** A man leaves his parents and in a public ceremony before God promises himself to his wife.
2. **Cleaving:** The man and the woman are joined together in the sight of God and take responsibility for each other's welfare and to love each other above all others.
3. **Weaving:** The two become one flesh in the act of intimacy which is reserved for marriage and not beforehand.

A strong marriage includes all of these. This is not my say so it is God's say so.

Time does not stand still but love must blaze new trails overcoming all the irritations, major problems, little heartaches and tremendous sorrows into a bright new day tomorrow together. When I do this, I do it in the knowledge that my lover is with me every step of the way and every trial and tribulation is worth it all for the one I love.

Solomon was able, under the inspiration of God, to write and express this love better than me. He wrote regarding the girl in love in Song of Solomon 8:6-7, "*... for love is strong as death; jealousy is cruel as the grave: the coals thereof are coals of fire, which hath a most vehement flame. Many waters cannot quench love, neither can the floods drown it: if a man would give all the substance of his house for love, it would utterly be contemned.*"

In the ancient near East it was improper for a young girl to express her love in public except among family members. The girl we read of in this passage wishes with all her heart she could express freely her affections for her lover in the public place. In this final account of their love together the girl adds some of the outstanding characteristics of this love. She states that love is as strong as death and cannot be killed by time or disaster. Too, it cannot be purchased for any price because it is freely given. Love is beyond price and even the richest king or queen cannot buy it.

Our Queen's grandson, Prince Harry, was married on the May 19, 2018. Money was not a problem here and I would expect that no expense was spared in giving the couple their dream wedding. The world was talking about the 'wedding of the year'. The couple did seem to be greatly in love, and I wish them well but what about the "Wedding of all time and eternity"? What about when Christ returns for His bride is the bride prepared and ready? Are you and I ready?

Love must be accepted as a gift from God and then shared within the guidelines that God gives you and me. I accept the love of my husband as God's gift to me and I strive to make my love a reflection of the perfect love (Agape love) that comes from God Himself.

God forms and equips men and woman for various tasks, but all these tasks lead to the same purpose which is to honour God. A husband and wife's talents and abilities should complement each other and as one they then bring glory and honour to God. Man gives life to the woman and woman brings life into the world. That are the fruits of a marriage. That fruit in turn is to bring glory to God. Does that happen in present day marriages? Sadly, in the majority of cases it does not. Ian and I strive each day to do so but we can only do so by the grace of God.

Thank God that with the love He imparts to me I can say I love my husband as much today as the day I married him. I do not want to give a moment's thought to being separated from him by death. It would be nice if we were to be taken together in death, but it would be glorious if we were to live and see Christ return for His bride.

The Great Royal Wedding

"Husbands, love your wives, even as Christ also loved the church, and gave himself for it; That he might sanctify and cleanse it with the washing of water by the word, That he might present it to himself a glorious church, not having spot, or wrinkle, or any such thing; but that

it should be holy and without blemish. So ought men to love their wives as their own bodies. He that loveth his wife loveth himself. For no man ever yet hated his own flesh; but nourisheth and cherisheth it, even as the Lord the church: For we are members of his body, of his flesh, and of his bones. For this cause shall a man leave his father and mother, and shall be joined unto his wife, and they two shall be one flesh. This is a great mystery: but I speak concerning Christ and the church."
Ephesians 5:25-32

Interspersed in this practical section dealing with relationships are some of the most significant truths relating to Christ's love for and connection to the Church found in the Bible.

There is a mysterious link between a human marriage and a relationship with Christ. In this passage, Paul assimilates from the mysterious unity in a marriage to the mysterious unity of Christ and the Church. I want to look at this briefly.

a) Jesus loves the Church. His love motivates Him to sanctify or treat the Church as special. That sanctification comes about by the application of His Word. He actively participates in the growth of the Church in order that he might enjoy a vital relationship.

He focuses on the splendour of the Church. He works toward the church's purity (without spot or wrinkle, holy and blameless). He nourishes and cherishes the Church. He is vitally connected with the Church; we are members of His body.

b) Husbands love wives who are to respect them.
Husbands are called to love their wives in the same way

as Christ loves the Church. Husbands are to love their wives as they would their own selves. This oneness is the core of marriage.

Paul includes a quote from the Old Testament that was also quoted by Jesus in the Gospels. The quote originally appears in the book of Genesis after joining Adam and Eve. (I have mentioned it above.) It's a phrase we have probably heard many times.

> *"Therefore a man shall leave his father and mother and hold fast to his wife, and the two shall become one flesh."*
> Ephesians 5:31

Here's the context of the original quote. God provided a 'helpmeet' (woman) for Adam. God caused a deep sleep to fall upon the man, and while he slept took one of his ribs and closed up its place with flesh. And the rib that the LORD God had taken from the man he made into a woman and brought her to Adam who then named her 'woman' Eve.

The duty of husbands is to love their wives. The love of Christ to the Church is an example, which is sincere, pure, and constant, notwithstanding her failures. Christ gave Himself for the Church, that he might sanctify it in this world, and glorify it in the next, that He might bestow on all His members a principle of holiness, and deliver them from the guilt, the pollution, and the dominion of sin, by those influences of the Holy Spirit, of which baptismal water was the outward sign.

Remember the three basic actions required to secure a sound marriage? Let me tell you it is exactly the same in the great marriage to the KING of Kings. You and I must obey the Word of God in our spiritual marriage. How do I do this?

I must:

Leave my family and friends to unite with Christ. When I invited Jesus Christ into my heart, I effectively said I now acknowledge Christ as my Lord and Saviour and He is my everything. He is number one no matter what. If it comes to a choice of putting Christ or family first, I will always put Christ first. I did not always do this as you have seen but I now have learned from my mistakes and seek to hold Him Lord of my life.

Cleave to Christ through thick and thin. Because of His great love for me unconditionally I love Him with all my being. For me it is choosing to leave the world and the things of the world behind me and clinging to Christ. It is not a sacrifice but devotion for my Lord. The things I did, the places I went and the company I kept, if it was not Christian, I chose to turn my back on it. "Forsaking all others" it is Christ for me my hope and glory.

Weave sons and daughters into the family of God. When Christ washed me in His precious Blood, He not only saved me, but He saved me to serve. This is the same for you also. Everyone is saved to serve but not all in the same job or field. Not of me but by the mercies of God I seek to share the gospel with the people I meet every day both at home and internationally. My goal and desire are to 'birth' new sons and daughters into the family of God and to 'mother' those already born. I seek to feed the babies pure milk till they are ready to be weaned; then to feed them the mana and meat which is the unadulterated Word of God. Why? Because this is the command of God found in 1Corinthians 3:1-2, *"And I, brethren, could not speak unto you as unto spiritual, but as unto carnal, even as unto babes in Christ. I have fed you with milk, and not with meat: for hitherto ye were not able to bear it, neither yet now are ye able."*

When a baby is born it must be fed pure milk as it is not strong enough to cope with anything more but as it grows the diet gradually changes. The milk lays down the early foundation but if a baby was to stay on milk it would not develop properly.

> *"As newborn babes, desire the sincere milk of the word, that ye may grow thereby:"* 1 Peter 2:2

> *"For when for the time ye ought to be teachers, ye have need that one teach you again which be the first principles of the oracles of God; and are become such as have need of milk, and not of strong meat. For every one that useth milk is unskilful in the word of righteousness: for he is a babe. But strong meat belongeth to them that are of full age, even those who by reason of use have their senses exercised to discern both good and evil."* Hebrews 5:12-14

If a babe in Christ is in a church that is not giving true teaching, then that babe will not grow and develop as he or she should. You and I need solid meat with all the vitamins and minerals in our daily diet. This in the spiritual is getting into God's Holy Word and studying it carefully under the inspiration of God. Just as a child needs to be trained to know and partake of a healthy diet so you and I need to understand and partake of good bible study methods and a good prayer life.

Our teacher is the Holy Spirit and we receive the Holy Spirit when we commit our life to Christ and invite the Holy Spirit in to take control. Under the guidance and direction of the Holy Spirit you and I will grow in grace and in love. Sad to say many pulpits are occupied by people to whom rigormortis has set in. They never got past sipping a little milk. As each day passed the strength faded from their body and they became like one that was dead.

If you are spiritually dead reading this, wake up! There is yet time! Seek the Lord while He may be found and repent of your evil ways *today*!

Marriage is more than a Wedding Service. Relationships need work over time. At the beginning you and I might expect a new husband to bound effortlessly from the bed, throw back the curtains and exclaim to his wife, "Lo, the morn". Over time the passion can dissipate. Perhaps you or I will drag ourselves out from under the blankets, pull the curtain and say, "Mow the lawn".

You and I need to learn to live together — as man and wife. James says in James 1:19; "*Wherefore, my beloved brethren, let every man be swift to hear, slow to speak, slow to wrath:*" One of the best things you and I can do for the future of our marriage is to maintain a spirit of thankfulness. Every day give thanks for our partner and avoid being critical. If you need God's help for this then ask! My earthly marriage to Ian is lovely. Not always an easy road over the forty-seven years but with Ian as my husband all was possible to face. My spiritual union with Christ is the ultimate state for me. It will be the greatest day of all when I am called to partake of the marriage supper of the Lamb in glory.

This is a great foundation for any marriage. There is much more you and I can learn, from God's book, the Bible, now that God has brought our partner to us in marriage.

Purpose Filled & Praise Driven

A life that is filled with the Lord's purpose and driven by praise will cause God to count me worthy of my calling. He will fulfil my every desire for goodness and empower my work with faith.

There are three things that each person, either consciously or unconsciously, wishes to strive for. They are health, wealth and wisdom. However, I want to look at them from a spiritual point of view.

1. Health - MOT
2. Wealth - Not earthly
3. Wisdom - Wisdom of God

Health

My son Derek is a vintage mini car fanatic. He lives eats and sleeps mini cars. Although he does not live with us, he has a great big garage and workshop in our yard. After finishing four years at university in England and graduating, he worked for only a few years. Unfortunately, he had sustained a back injury whilst in England which turned out to be debilitating. Not able to follow his career on strong medical advice and not being one to sit and twiddle his thumbs, so to speak, he needed something to occupy his mind and hands. Thus, he bought two old minis. One had a good engine but rotten shell and the other had a reasonable shell but not so good an engine.

Derek's plan was to swap the engines and refurbish the whole car. Where would a young man commence this project keeping in mind, he had no mechanical knowledge whatsoever?

1. The first thing to do was to take time out and do some research into putting together a plan of action.
2. When he drew up his plan of action, he needed to gather together the knowhow to execute each step.
3. He needed to make a list of all tools and machinery he would require and assess what he would buy and what he would have to hire.
4. He needed to come alongside a like-minded person who had the same passion for minis as he had.
5. Last, but not least, he had to be teachable and be willing to learn from the man with all the experience and skills.

Derek is a very conscientious young man and anything he does he will always do it to the very best of his ability. He strives for perfection at all times. I must confess I had grave doubts regarding his ability to restore and old vintage mini, but I never spoke my fleeting thoughts but chose always to encourage him. It is a case of 'like mother like son'.

Through life I worked hard to prove that a person can achieve anything if they set their mind to it. When working in my career I often said, "anything a man can do a woman can do twice as well." A strange statement you might think but I seemed to always be in the very small minority in the workplace as I was often the only female in a male dominated industry. On reflection I think I stated this more to encourage myself than to stir some 'banter' amongst my male colleagues. I firmly believe and live by the principle that grades don't measure intelligence and age doesn't define maturity.

Time has passed since Derek embarked on his project and by the time this book goes to print his mini will be on the road and driven in the Northern Ireland Mini Club vintage rally. With much reading on mechanical engineering and enormous hands on teaching from his two professional and experienced friends, William and Ronnie, Derek has come a long way.

We were sitting one evening and Derek was explaining the work he had just completed and problems that he had encountered along the way. He then explained how he had methodically gone through each step to rule out any mistakes he had made until he had isolated the problem to a particular part.

I got to thinking generally about a car and the more I thought upon the workings and mechanics to having a 'sweet running' and reliable car the more I saw the comparison to the human body. The car is the human body; the manufacturer is not Toyota, Nissan, Ford, or such like, but God is the Creator; the mechanic is to the car what the doctor is to the human body and the Holy Spirit is to the spiritual body. With this thought I want to carry on and look at what a good mechanic does when he services a car going for a MOT. The purpose of a MOT check here in the United Kingdom is to carefully inspect a car to see that all the vital parts are in good condition and will carry the passengers safely as intended by the manufacturer. Vehicles that are three years of age and over must have a MOT inspection yearly. If the vehicle passes the inspection there is a MOT certificate issued on the spot and that vehicle is deemed road worthy. It can be taxed and insured to drive on the public highway. If the vehicle fails the MOT inspection, there will be a failure notice given which lists why it has failed and that vehicle may not be legally driven until the repairs are done and resubmitted for a further inspection. Only when it passes the second or perhaps even the third time will the owner be given a certificate enabling them to tax and insure the vehicle.

The mechanic also checks that all parts which are vital to the 'sweet running' of the engine are replaced. This sounds very similar to my yearly visit to the doctor. And that is exactly what I as a child of God need on a very regular basis so that I may serve the purposes God created me for.

I do not profess to be a mechanic, but I did ask my son when a customer brings a car what all he does to that vehicle in checking and preparing it to pass a MOT test. The list is long but each point worth looking at briefly. It is in no particular order.

Air filter: The air filter catches all the dust and dirt preventing it from going into the engine. The filter is taken out and replaced with a new one to ensure the engine is 'breathing' easily and does not get congested.

The air filter to the car is the same as my lungs are to me. When I go to the Doctor for my yearly check-up, which is often referred to as a MOT also, the doctor will take a stethoscope and check my lungs. He can tell if I am able to breathe easy. Sometimes I may feel a little short of breath and I would have to take medication to correct the problem.

In the Spiritual I need to be breathing in clear pure breath. It comes from God breathing on me. I often have read and sung in church the hymn: Breathe on me, breath of God and I believe it encapsulate everything in the verses:

Breathe on me, Breath of God,
Fill me with life anew,
That I may love what Thou dost love,
And do what Thou wouldst do.

Breathe on me, Breath of God,
Until my heart is pure,
Until with Thee I will one will,
To do and to endure.

Breathe on me, Breath of God,
Till I am wholly Thine,
Until this earthly part of me
Glows with Thy fire divine.

Breathe on me, Breath of God,
So shall I never die,
But live with Thee the perfect life
Of Thine eternity.

By Edwin Hatch 1878 Published by Robert Jackson 1888
Copyright is Public Domain

There is nothing I can do for God or in His ministry without the Holy Spirit in me. It is the Holy Spirit that guides, directs, teaches and speaks through me. I have to be found in the place where the Holy Spirit has free access in my life.

Oil Filter and change of Oil. I am told these two things go together. A good mechanic will do an oil change if he sees that the oil is thin or getting low. But the mechanic will not stop there but will also change the oil filter. The oil filter does just as the name suggests and filters the oil. Any mechanic will tell you after a certain number of miles it is advisable to carry out an oil and filter change. As the oil moves around the engine the filter will catch any dirt that may have got gathering and also little steel filing that can come from the engine. There is absolutely no point in putting new oil in and leaving a dirty filter. It defeats the whole purpose of doing the oil change.

Therefore, when a car is being serviced it is always important to change the oil and the oil filter. Often the oil filter is black, and the oil has gone very thin after many miles have been covered. If it is getting bad the engine can start to make a noise which should prompt the driver to stop and check. The performance of the engine is greatly compromised until the change has been done. The oil filter collects any small filings or dirt that may be collected in the oil as it circulates the engine. As the oil passes through the filter it is 'cleansed' and so is good to go on circulating. The oil lubricates the engine and if the oil goes very low or thin the engine will become heated and can even seize or blow up. If that happens then it means the car is parked up until a new engine is purchased and fitted. If the car is up in years it just may have to be scrapped instead. At the very least there will have been serious damaged caused.

How like us? The oil to the car is what the blood in our veins is to you and me. The doctor will take our blood pressure and check our heart by listening to it. He can tell a great deal by the sounds he hears. An irregular heartbeat, a racing heart or perhaps the heart is struggling. The heart may be under pressure to keep pumping the blood around the body and a high blood pressure reading will indicate this. It may also come from impurities in the blood. The doctor will also have blood samples taken to check for any abnormalities. If I am feeling very tired it could be a result of a low blood count and I need my blood level brought up or I could have some other blood related problem. The doctor knows that blood tests will reveal many conditions. However, if I have high cholesterol which can clog the arteries this can lead to a heart attack which will stop me there and then. A clot moving along and reaching the heart will cause a fatal heart attack. If the problem is caught early enough surgery can save a life by the surgeon inserting new valves. It is not uncommon for someone to receive a new heart or have open heart surgery. It is only when the person neglects themselves or does not heed the warning signs that it can be fatal.

A doctor will have done blood tests and he will look at what the blood test results reveal and flag up any obvious potential problems. The blood filters toxins out of the system. It will show raised or high cholesterol levels; the same for sugar levels; problems with the liver or kidney function as well as the haemoglobin level. If the blood count is very low, they can arrange for a blood transfusion. As for all the other problems revealed if caught early enough it may mean just a change in diet or if necessary, a course of medication. Healthy blood readings mean the body is not being put under pressure or stress to try and perform at its best.

How like the spiritual this is. By nature, we are born in sin and it is often referred to as having a black heart — sin has caused the heart to be black. You and I have to come to a realisation that we are sinners before we can know the Holy Spirit living in us. When God convicted me of my sin and sinful way of life, He did it by sending the Holy Spirit to arrest my conscious. I heard the old, old story of how Jesus left his home in glory and came to earth to die on Calvary so that I could go free. When I asked Jesus to forgive me and come into my life and live in me and wash me in His precious Blood, He did just that. It was like suffering a heart attack. I realised my need of a Saviour but could do nothing but cry out to Christ to save me. He did open-heart surgery and removed my dirty black heart and gave me a new heart for Christ. The blood in me was no longer contaminated because the Holy Spirit came in and I was given a spiritual blood transfusion. The old was removed and the new was poured in.

Just like the chorus often sung based on Luke 10:30-34 (KJV), "*And Jesus answering said, A certain man went down from Jerusalem to Jericho, and fell among thieves, which stripped him of his raiment, and wounded him, and departed, leaving him half dead. And by chance there came down a certain priest that way: and when he saw him, he passed by on the other side. And likewise a Levite, when he was at the place, came and looked on him, and passed by on the other side. But a certain Samaritan, as he journeyed, came where he was: and when he saw him, he had compassion on him, And went to him, and bound up his wounds, pouring in oil and wine, and set him on his own beast, and brought him to an inn, and took care of him.*"

Chorus
He poured in the oil and the wine
The kind that restoreth my soul
He found me bleeding and dying on the Jericho Road
And He poured in the oil and the wine.
(author unknown)

Jesus Christ came to me and bound up my wounds which sin had made. It is part of the work of Christ, to bind up the broken-hearted, to heal wounded sinners, and restore comforts to those who are down and at 'wits end corner'. He does this by pouring in oil and wine: by which generally is meant and understood to be the Blood of Christ, applied to the conscience of a wounded sinner; which cleanses from all sin, heals all the wounds and diseases of sin, cheers and revives fainting spirits, gives ease, peace, and pleasure, and is therefore exceedingly valuable and precious. What a precious gift Christ gave to me. I had a blood problem and God had a blood solution. It's all about the blood and nothing but the blood.

Unlike the car that needed a new engine my new 'engine' was provided through the great sacrifice of Christ on the cross. He paid for it all and my bill was marked 'Paid in full'. When Christ arose and ascended to the Father in heaven the comforter, the Holy Spirit was sent to dwell in the child of God. My new oil was now the Holy Spirit living in me. As I move to the Spiritual, I can now understand the function and work of the Holy Spirit. Oil represents the Holy Spirit and if the Holy Spirit does not have free course in me, I am not able to live to my full potential in the Lord. When I was saved, I found that was only the beginning of my new journey and as I grew, I came to know that great men and woman in the ministry could only function fully when they experienced the infilling of the Holy Spirit. I prayed earnestly for this and one day I was baptised by the Holy Spirit with the evidence of speaking in tongues. This is what the Lord promised His disciples when he fellowshipped with them after His resurrection but prior to His ascension.

> *"And, (Jesus) being assembled together with them, commanded them that they should not depart from Jerusalem, but wait for the promise of the Father, which, saith he, ye have heard of me. For John truly baptized with water; but ye shall be baptized with the Holy Ghost not many days hence....But ye shall receive power, after that the Holy Ghost is come upon you: and ye shall be witnesses unto me both in Jerusalem, and in all Judaea, and in Samaria, and unto the uttermost part of the earth."* Acts 1:4-5, 8

Our Lord had told the disciples the exact ministry they were to be active in. The apostles had met together at Jerusalem; Christ had commanded them not to depart from Jerusalem but to wait for the pouring out of the Holy Spirit. This would be the coming of the comforter, the Holy Spirit, giving them a supernatural power to work miracles, and enlightening and sanctifying their souls. This baptism of the Holy Spirit would confirm the Divine promise to the apostles, and it was a means to encourage and assure them. It was to take away all fear and doubt of being alone without Christ to walk alongside them. This promise also encourages us to depend upon it too, because we have heard it from Christ; for in Him all the promises of God are yea and amen. I read this and I understood it so I was keen to claim the promise and to have this baptism as others before me had experienced.

On the Day of Pentecost, the Holy Spirit was made available to all who believed in Jesus. We all, but specifically me, would receive the Holy Spirit if I waited praying and believing. The baptism of the Holy Spirit must be understood in the light of His complete work in Christians. The Holy Spirit marks the beginning of the Christian experience and it was to mark my growing and maturity in my spiritual journey. The power in a Christian's life comes only from the Holy Spirit dwelling in them. He begins a lifelong process of change as the child of God becomes more like Christ because when you or I receive Christ by faith we begin an immediate personal relationship with God. It is the Holy Spirit working in me that makes the change.

Jesus had promised the disciples in John 14:26 as follows; *"But the Comforter, which is the Holy Ghost, whom the Father will send in my name, he shall teach you all things, and bring all things to your remembrance, whatsoever I have said unto you."*

Jesus had instructed His disciples to witness to people of all nations about Him, but they were told to wait first for the Holy Spirit As mentioned in Luke 24:49; *"And, behold I send the promise of my Father: but tarry ye in the city of Jerusalem, until ye be endued with power from on high."* God has important work for me and for every child of God to do for Him, but I must do it by the power of the Holy Spirit. There can be no other way. I am guilty of often wanting to get on with the job even if it means running ahead of God. But waiting is sometimes part of God's plan. I need to ask you a question; are you waiting and listening for God's complete instructions or are you running ahead of His plans? We must have God's timing and power to be truly effective. It is enough that He has purposed to give believers strength equal to their trials and services; that under the influence of the Holy Spirit they may, in one way or other, be witnesses for Christ on earth, while in heaven He manages their concerns with perfect wisdom, truth, and love. This is what will ensure a happy and fulfilled life for any child of God and I am proving it in my own life as I serve the Lord. The life filled with the Holy Spirit will be guided in all things right down to their thinking and speech and will result in living life to a high level.

People were to know immediately there had been a change in me because the old Eileen had been dying inside. I had been living and talking about things of the world and doing things of the world. But the Eileen, the Eileen who had just received heart surgery and new blood was alive and rejoicing night and day in her new-found faith. When the Holy Spirit comes in you or I can never remain the same. I was baptised later in the Spirit and was praying in tongues which brought me into sweet communion and closeness with God. I really was a new creation in Christ. Praise God!

It is true I will never be perfect until I reach Heaven. I sin daily but I have an advocate with the Father who is forever making intercession for me. Anything in my life that is not pleasing to God hinders the flow of the Holy Spirit. Therefore, I need to come before the Lord daily, kneel and ask for cleansing afresh. There must be nothing that hinders the flow of the Holy Spirit in me. Before we leave this point may I suggest to you that the word 'pour' suggests to me the effusing of the Blood of Christ and His grace and mercy into my life. What a lovely picture this brings to my mind.

Timing Belt. The timing belt is meant to be replaced every 5 years or every 75,000 miles whichever comes first. The timing belt co-ordinates all the functions of the engine and contributes much to the overall performance of the car. If the timing belt get stretch through wear or through age it starts to make a noise. If it snaps it will do much damage to the car engine.

In the physical it is like having a pacemaker fitted. The pacemaker regulates the heart and brings it back into normal function mode. If the heart was allowed to keep malfunctioning a heart attack could occur, but a pacemaker can actually give a man or woman a new lease of life again.

How like us in the spiritual sense. If I keep myself busy in ministry giving out without taking in from God, then I get stretched and start to lag and not give of my best in service. Sometimes it is just a case of same thing day in and day out that I can get into a routine and become blaze. There needs to be time where I come aside and rest in the Lord and allow Him to refresh my soul and thus refresh my ministry. I need to take regular time out to really study the Word for *me* — not for anyone else — but for me to get back in tune with the Lord and to know exactly His will for my life. That includes prayer time as well.

Brakes. Brakes are so important on the car. It is good to have a good or even high-performance car but while the driver likes to drive fast he needs to know that when he approaches a road end, traffic light, or to avoid a collision when he needs to do an emergency stop, that he has good and reliable breaks. If he was to hit the brakes and found them to fail the consequence could at best be life changing and worst fatal for him or someone else.

The doctor will, when I am in for a check-up, test my reflexes. This indicates how sharp I am in my reactions and if I will be able to save myself from trips, falls, or if something was to suddenly happen, I could react quickly to save myself from injury.

God has built into each one of us a conscious that will be pricked when things are not right in our life. Furthermore, I have found as a child of God, when I prayed for God to give me discernment, He did just that. When something or someone is not as it should be, I have a witness in my spirit, and I know to be careful and extricate myself from that person or place.

An example of this was when I met a man in Uganda who claimed to be a pastor. When I was in his company, I always felt very uncomfortable and on edge. Anything he said or did I was analysing it immediately. My guard was up, and I could never relax. I spoke with Pastor Godfrey and expressed my grave concerns. He was feeling the very same. We prayed and asked God to cover us with the Blood of Christ and reveal all things to us. Sure enough, God revealed to us the man was a false teacher and was trying to con money from the 'white woman'. Praise God for discernment. It truly is a gift from God.

Tyre and tyre pressure. If any of the tyres are worn down or damaged, they must be replaced, and all the tyres pressures checked to make sure they are at the correct pressure.

When I go to the doctor regarding a problem in or on my feet, he will check my feet, and in some cases, may suggest a change of shoes or perhaps just something fitted in the shoe to take the shock out of the contact with the ground. How often have you and I heard people ask, 'how on earth can they walk in shoes like that"?

This brings to mind Ephesians 6:15, which tell me that as a child of God what type of shoes I am to wear; *"And your feet shod with the preparation of the gospel of peace..."*

What does this really mean? It means for me to stand my ground or to be able to march forward in rugged paths, my feet must be shod with the preparation of the gospel of peace. Motives to obedience, amidst trials, must be drawn from a clear knowledge of the gospel. Those are the shoes I need to wear to be able to walk the road that God has put me on. If I have the wrong shoes on, I will slip and slide and fall for anything. Friend, I cannot and will not allow that to happen to me. With God's help and by His grace and mercy I will wear the shoes of the gospel. I will take the gospel to anywhere the Lord opens the door in the world for me to go through.

Lights and Indicators. The light and indicators are minor parts of the car but are essential for safe driving not only for the diver but also for other road users. The lights are required to give the driver a clear vision in a dark world at night time. Also, it allows and oncoming car driver to see and know where exactly the other vehicle is in the road. The lights need to be set correctly. If they are to high, they will blind the vision of the oncoming person and if they are dim it may cause the driver to have an accident or to not be seen.

The indicators are there so that the driver can 'indicate' his intentions to those on the road around him.

When I go and have my eyes checked the doctor will assess if I require glasses or if there is any problems with my eyesight. I may have a crooked eye and though I may appear to be looking straight ahead I am actually seeing in a different direction. If my eyes are dim, I cannot see well enough to read. I might be short sighted or even long sighted but whatever I will be advised, and the corrective measures will be taken.

If this then is the case in the natural how much more is it true in the spiritual? How often have I heard preachers pray for 20/20 spiritual vision? You may have heard a pastor pray for God to open the eyes of the listeners as he comes to preach the Word. We need our spiritual eyes to be in excellent condition. I need my eyes open to the things of God and to see people without Christ who are perishing and on their way to hell. I need to see the love Christ has for sinners and to go tell them Christ is standing with His arms outstretched waiting to receive them. It is not for me to shine my light to blind them but rather that they will see Christ in me.

> *"Ye are the light of the world. A city that is set on an hill cannot be hid."* Matthew 5:14

My light must shine so the world will see Christ. It is not to be an ordinary light but such a bright light that people can see it from a far off and nothing going on in the world can hide it. I need to have all my lights clear and showing that people know exactly where I am on the road, where I am heading and what exactly I intend to do or moves I intend to make before even I make them.

An example of this is the debate on abortion that is continually on the lips of our politicians at present. I would like to believe that everyone who knows me has talked to me or sat under my teaching and preaching would know that I stand four square on the Word of God on this matter. That I believe the scriptures in Jeremiah 1:5; *"Before I formed thee in the belly I knew thee; and before thou camest forth out of the womb I sanctified thee..."* This means that God has a plan and purpose for each life. Murder is murder and there is no argument that can stand against this. You nor I cannot and must not play God. The Lord gives life and the Lord takes life away. Blessed be the name of the Lord.

There is something else about the eyes that I wish to bring here briefly. It is eye trouble of a different kind. It is 'I' trouble not 'eye' trouble and there is much of it to be found in the Church.

'I' know who she's talking about — the 'I' of pride. Apply it to your life first. Search your heart.

'I' don't agree with all she says — the 'I' of dissention. Don't agree with me but with God's Word.

'I' was not taught that when I was growing up — the 'I' of superiority. You need to align your heart soul mind and body to the teaching of God.

There is only room for one 'I' in the Church and that is the 'Great I Am'. A good study would be to check out all the "I Am's of Christ.

There is much more I could go into when comparing the servicing of a car to the natural man and ultimately to the spiritual man, but I trust this will suffice to enable you to see that in everything God speaks to us in the natural and then He speaks to us in the spiritual. It is necessary to keep fully serviced so that you and I can be totally effective in our everyday living as a servant of the Lord.

I need to keep regular checks on my health and so do you. But it is much more important to keep regular checks on my spiritual health. It is so easy to become complacent, but all satan needs is a little slip from me, a lack of attention of my spiritual body and welfare and he will soon reap havoc in my life. I cannot afford to let that happen because, just like the car, the more that is permitted to go wrong and stay wrong the harder it is to repair and get back to a worthy condition. Better to not even go there than to take a chance and experience ruin.

Tried, Tested and Protected

D. L. Moody is reported to have said, "The best way to revive a church is to light a fire in the pulpit." That is of course God's fire.

We have people up and down the land praying for revival and amazed that it is not happening in the land. My question to them would be: why? I believe if we were to stop and examine ourselves first and then the churches, we would get the answer loud and clear. We need to get revived ourselves by getting back to the God of our Salvation. I need and you need to go back to our first love of Jesus Christ and ask forgiveness and get in a close relationship with Him again and then things will start to happen.

However, for this chapter I want to look at the problems in the church and mainly in the pulpits. The verse that I hold close to here is found in 1 John 4:1; *"Beloved, believe not every spirit, but try the spirits whether they are of God: because many false prophets are gone out into the world."*

What John is telling me here is: Don't be easily taken in; don't be easily led. The old proverb is true: all that glitters is not gold.

I was up at the great Nile falls and when I arrived and got out of the land-rover I was stunned to see all the ground around me glittering in the sunshine. I asked the young man, Martin, what it was as I bent down and lifted some small pieces of rock to inspect more closely. It was so beautiful, and I thought I had just discovered something really special and valuable. Imagine my shock when Martin told me it was 'fool's gold'. I turned it and viewed it from every angle. It was stunning and I just loved it. I started to gather a few more small pieces of rock, but Martin exclaimed quickly, "Oh, don't take that stuff. It is not real gold but fool's gold and not worth anything." Well, to be honest I did not care that it was worthless I just wanted some samples to bring back to show people back home and illustrate some of my studies. Beautiful to look at! To the untrained eye it looked expensive – the real thing, but to the expert it was only stuff that fools went after – totally worthless.

How like what we find today in many churches; a religion but not the gospel of Jesus Christ. I want to look at what God is saying to me in his Holy Word. At the end of the day it is not important what I think or what any person thinks. God speaks through the Bible and when I read the scriptures, I am warned what to look out for and what to avoid.

Test the Spirits
"Beloved, believe not every spirit, but try the spirits whether they are of God: because many false prophets are gone out into the world. Hereby know ye the Spirit of God: Every spirit that confesseth that Jesus Christ is come in the flesh is of God: And every spirit that confesseth not that Jesus Christ is come in the flesh is not of God: and this is that spirit of antichrist, whereof ye have heard that it should come; and even now already it is in the world." 1John 4:1-6

Matthew Henry said this: "Preaching is not designed to teach us something new in every sermon; but to put us in remembrance, to call to mind things forgotten. Though you know these things, you still need to know them better."

If I consider first the time John was in when he wrote this book under the influence of the Holy Spirit, I read that the church was faced with much wrong teaching. There were many false prophets who were spreading wrong teaching across the world. As this verse implies, these false prophets were claiming that they were inspired by the Spirit of God. Yet, they were teaching a totally wrong and anti-scriptural message.

In an earlier chapter John had just explained to the believers that they know Christ abides in them and they abide in Him because of the Spirit whom Christ has given them. Now, in this verse, John exhorts the believers to "test the spirits to see whether they are from God." He not only exhorts or urges them to test the spirits. He does not leave it there, but he tells them and thus everyone since who reads the Bible, the method and test to use to check these various spirits.

I must say here that not all spirits are bad. Some of the spirits mentioned here are from God but others are definitely not. I learn something interesting in this and that is that both types of spirits speak. Of course, this is referring to the false prophets and the believers.

False prophets: Beware!

In John's day, but I believe more so today, there were many false prophets. They are masquerading as wolves in sheep's clothing. It is an evil spirit from the devil himself that is inspiring the false prophets. They are against Christ and do not recognise or confess Him as their Lord and Saviour.

If you or I were to speak with them or conduct an interview, we would find they do not have a personal relationship with Jesus Christ. I remember visiting with a Bishop in his home and I asked him how he received his call to the ministry. Imagine my reaction when he told me that as the first son of a middle-class family it was automatically assumed that he should go into the church. Just a job to him – there was no calling.

Even today, as in the ancient church, many evil forces are arrayed against Christ. One of the most common and serious misconceptions of the day is that there are many roads to Salvation and Heaven. The deity of Christ and His atoning death as the Son of God is denied. That Salvation can be found in no other is not recognised. How often I have heard ministers say, "God is a God of love and He will not sent anyone to hell." God has given man a free choice and it is man who chooses to go to hell by denying his or her need of forgiveness as a hell deserving sinner and coming by faith to the foot of the old rugged cross where there they will find that the Blood of Jesus Christ cleanses us from all sin.

> *"If we say that we have no sin, we deceive ourselves, and the truth is not in us. If we confess our sins, he is faithful and just to forgive us* our *sins, and to cleanse us from all unrighteousness."* 1John 1:8-9

The false prophets and apostates do not believe this, and they certainly never preach this gospel but that is what this world's people need to be warned against.

This then helps us with the first test which has to do with the confession of the believers. The believers are inspired by the Spirit of truth, the Holy Spirit. However, as I have said, there are good as well as evil spirits. The good spirits, the believers, are in tune with and walking in the Spirit of truth. The believers gladly confess that Jesus Christ is God the Son and He came to earth taking on the form of man to live and then to die on the cross of Calvary for the sins of the world.

Many of the false prophets either minimized or opposed the idea that Christ came in the flesh, but John clearly states that this is not true, and he presents the basic gospel truths. Thus, I see behind these words John urging me to know the truth that I must, and need believe. There are three things for you and me to note the first being that the man Jesus of Nazareth is indeed the divine Word of God. Secondly that Jesus Christ was and is fully divine as well as human; and thirdly that Jesus is the only source of eternal life. He alone reveals the Father to us and He alone atones for our sins.

In verse 5 of chapter 4 John states, *"They are of the world: therefore speak they of the world, and the world heareth them."* This is the second test and it has to do with who is listening to the messages being preached. John shows that the false prophets, the apostates and the world are in perfect agreement. Those who listens and enjoys the teachings of the false prophets are of the world. In complete contrast to the apostates and false prophets are the true teachers that are from God. The man or woman boy or girl who knows God will always want to listen to the true teaching and preaching of Godly preachers. Many preachers today occupy the pulpits, but few are actually called of God.

It is the Holy Spirit that inspires the true preachers. They will not be preaching sugary coated and syrupy sermons that will tickle the ears of their congregation and not prick their conscious. No, I know when I prepare a message that the Holy Spirit lays on my heart it is always to challenge the believer, stir the hearts of the unbeliever and the Holy

Spirit will convict them of sin. Then if I have been faithful to God, when I give an altar call the Holy Spirit will have been working and He will do all the rest. When God's Spirit inspires a preacher, the people will discern God's truth and there will be fruit for the labour.

I love what John says in verse 4; "*Ye are of God, little children, and have overcome them: because greater is he that is in you, than he that is in the world.*" What he says is that the believers have overcome the false teachers and also have overcome the world. God abides in them, and He is greater than he who is in the world. God is greater than satan, 'He that is in the world'. The Greek reads '*ho entoi kosmoi*', which really interprets as the prince of this world, the god of this world.

Because of this, he exhorted the church to tests the spirits. Today, the church encounters a great deal of false doctrine and teaching. As in the days of John, we must always rely on the basic truths of the Gospel. Now, we have the New Testament in its full form. The Word of God is our surest guide to the truth.

My calling, as a teacher and pastor, is to be the preacher that preaches the counsel of God. It is to be the shepherd that promotes a concern for the proper condition of the church. In addition, the calling of the preacher and so mine also is to practice preventative procedures by being a watchman.

In Jude 3-4 it is written, "*Beloved, when I gave all diligence to write unto you of the common salvation, it was needful for me to write unto you, and exhort you that ye should earnestly contend for the faith which was once delivered unto the saints. For there are certain men crept in unawares, who were before of old ordained to this condemnation, ungodly men, turning the grace of our God into lasciviousness, and denying the only Lord God, and our Lord Jesus Christ."*

I want you and I to think about Jude's use of the word diligence. He states, *"when I gave all diligence."* Diligence means: Steady application in business of any kind; constant effort to accomplish what is undertaken; exertion of body or mind without unnecessary delay or sloth; due attention; industry; assiduity. It also means: Care; heed; heedfulness. Proverbs 4:23, *"Keep thy heart with all diligence; for out of it are the issues of life."* We need diligence in our Christian lives. We seem to understand diligence in other areas, but let it slip in our spiritual lives. I submit to you today that diligence is required in our Christian lives – in your life and in mine.

Diligence is required in living for God, looking for God, labouring for God and lasting the course for God. If we are going to continue, we must be diligent. We cannot give up. We cannot quit. We cannot take a leave of absence. We must continue forward. The time for rest will be later. The time for relaxation will be over on the other side. Praise God!

Jude wanted to write about the common Salvation. He wanted to give a treatise for the wonderful grace of Jesus, but instead was instructed to plead for the saints to earnestly contend for the faith. Not just a generic faith, but the faith that was once delivered to the saints. He not only was writing but exhorting them about this faith. The word once is the Greek word *'haxpa'*. This word carries the idea of a once for all. It is not a faith that is different today than it was two thousand years ago. It is the same faith, yesterday, today, and forever.

This makes an interesting thought. Why do we read of men and women of God back in other eras of time who had more faith, greater commitment, and for more zeal for God than we find in our generation? It is because the warning from Jude to earnestly contend has been ignored. Today churches spend time making sure a sinner feels so comfortable with a little religion, that they do not need Christ. I look at all the new and modern gimmicks that are employed now to attract the people in. Sad to say in some of the churches today I would be hard pressed to know if I was not in some den of the devil than in a church. How sad is that? I, as a child of God, am called to be of this world but not in the world. I am called to be separated. There should be a marked and obvious difference. Earnestly contending simply carries the definition of struggling with an adversary. Through-out the rest of Jude we see Jude pleading with us to contend against the Apostates. Earnestly contending is trying to keep the saint away from the pack of dogs and out of the pig pen.

Jude is crying forth, sounding out like a trumpet- the war is on! There is a battle for what is right. There is a conflict going on within the walls of the church. Wake up and contend!!!

He is trying to get these first century followers of Christ to understand that there are apostates, pretenders, false prophets, claiming to be apostles. There were those who once named the name of Christ behaving like they had never encounter the saving grace of Jesus Christ. They were living their lives contrary to the teachings of both Jesus and His apostles. Another word for the false prophets is deceivers. These pretenders had gotten into the church under false pretences. They were deceivers. They were pretenders. They were crafty. They were wolves in sheep's clothing.

What was taking place was the thought that God had wiped away all their past sin. Thus, they were saved by the grace of God and they could live any way they desired. In other words, licentious living, living out the lusts of the flesh. It is the absence of moral restraints in behaviour.

Usually this individual will say to someone who has standards, "You are a legalist." You will not find that term in Scripture. The correct term found in Scripture is Pharisee. The Pharisees who thought they were more spiritual because they added things to the Bible.

I need to mention allowing the wrong music in the home. What is wrong with music, rock, country, jazz, rhythm and blues, rap, etc? We are not to fill our mind with the things of the world. Much of the music of today is talking about perverted love, affairs, one-night stands, drugs, alcohol, some form of illicit sexual activity. That is not for the Child of God. That is not to mention smoking, drinking, drugs, bars, men looking after a woman to lust, watching movies, and DVDs that have wicked behaviour on them and being endorsed.

This is the absence of moral restraint. These things end up in the church house. Why is it popular to let people dress inappropriately when coming to God's House? It is a lack of moral restraint. Why is the "anything goes" attitude so huge? It is a lack of moral restraint. I could go on and on...

The overwhelmingly popular trend in churches is to gratify people's carnality by making dress ultra-casual, ensuring that plenty of snacks and pastries are available, providing never-ending entertainment for all ages, allowing people to converse and move around as they please, and so on, but any honest reader of the Bible must surely conclude that this new tradition is contrary to the worship of God recorded and instructed in His Holy Word. More and more so the worship of the Lord in churches is being replaced by the traditions of man which revolve around worshipping self. In some churches here in the UK you could be forgiven for not knowing you are in a night club with the flashing coloured lights and smoke coming up on the stage around the singers and preacher. Such a church seems to be wildly popular. However, contrary to popular opinion, the Bible doesn't teach that churches are to mould and conform with society and man's opinions – what is 'politically correct' and does not offend the low morals of today – but rather to come out from among them and be ye separate.

There are Christians that really believe they never do anything wrong. They believe that everyone else is at fault. Everyone else is out to get them. They must always be doing it right, because of the persecution that seems to find its way to them. That makes great charismatic doctrine. That makes wonderful fertilizer to grow a garden of pride. But it is not biblical. God will punish those who abuse the grace of God to follow their own lusts. This is self-righteousness.

I must understand the seriousness of what the devil can accomplish and so must you. He can destroy our testimonies, he can destroy family relationships, he can destroy the churches, he can wreak havoc in our lives. I cannot play around as though the devil were nothing and neither can you. We need to resist this teaching from satan.

James 4:7 states, "*resist the devil and he will flee from you.*" Literally the word 'resist' means to stand against. Paul writing in Ephesians 6:11 and 13 says, "*Put on the whole armour of God, that ye may be able to stand against the wiles of the devil…Wherefore take unto you the whole armour of God, that ye may be able to withstand in the evil day, and having done all, to stand.*"

We are not to attack the devil. We are not to run from the devil. We are to stand fast and do all to stand.

There are three important words to remember in withstanding or resisting the devil. The first one is to pray. When the devil comes around it is a good time for me to talk to my Heavenly Father; to pray to Him and to let the devil know where my allegiance lies.

The second word is to praise. Hebrews 13:15, *"By him therefore let us offer the sacrifice of praise to God continually, that is, the fruit of our lips giving thanks to his name."*

By praising the Lord, you and I will not have time to listen to or be a part of what the devil wants. That is resisting the devil and his ways.

The third word is the 'Blood'. Not any blood but a Blood that has sin destroying power. Plead the Blood of Jesus Christ — by the Blood of the Lamb. Just begin to thank God for the Blood. The reason why churches and religious institutions have removed the Blood from their message and from their gospel is that they are sold out to the devil and his crowd. Remember, Eileen, it is still the Blood that saves from sin. I urge you, too, to remember this also.

There are those who have crept in the church unawares with some other way of salvation. Some say we are saved only by placing the Lord at the number one position of our heart. While He must occupy the throne of our heart, it is still the Blood that cleanses us from all unrighteousness. There are some who state it is only through the baptismal waters that one can be justified. If that were true, how could the thief on the cross be saved? There are those that believe it is by a series of good works that we can make it to Heaven. That at the end of life our good and bad will be weighed out and the good had better outweigh the bad. But the Scriptures indicate, *"Whosoever shall call upon the name of the Lord shall be saved."*

The Christian life is a separated life. There is to be a distinct difference between the way of God and the way of the devil. The closer I live to the Lord and the closer you live to the Lord the less we will desire the things of the world. The closer we get to the flame of His righteousness, the less we will desire the coldness of unrighteousness.

For the preacher and pastor this is what D.L. Moody meant when he stated, "The best way to revive a church is to light a fire in the pulpit." That is the preacher on fire with the Holy Ghost.

Let me share with you an experience of my own. It will serve to illustrate exactly the teaching of John and Jude. I often pray for God to never take from me the gift of discernment which He gave me. Many a time I have felt in my spirit that something is not as it appears and when I go with that, I thank God that it has always been the right decision.

I was in my office one day when I felt strongly that I should go and see a particular man and speak to him about his soul. I closed all down, lifted my things, and walked to the car. As I drove the 35 miles approximately to his home, I prayed the whole way that God would give me the words to speak and would use me in whatever way He wished. It is important to allow the Holy Spirit to guide in all things.

When the man opened the door to me, he was surprised to see me. As I shared with him how I felt prompted to come and speak with him regarding his soul he invited me in. The gospel message is very simple that even a child can understand it and I shared the simple truths and said how God must really love him to have someone come and tell him his need of Salvation. The man broke down in tears and told me he had been trying to put God off for a long time and had asked God to send him someone to tell him how he could be saved. Imagine the joy in my heart as I led that man to Jesus Christ and with tears running down his cheeks, he prayed a simple pray of repentance and in faith asked Jesus into his heart and then trusted for his forgiveness of sins.

What if I had not acted on what I had discerned? Thank God He impressed on my heart so strongly to leave work and go see that man. Thank God I recognised the Holy Spirit's prompting.

However, the most remarkable time I saw discernment really at work was in Africa. It was one of my earlier trips and Pastor Godfrey Mugolo was with me as I travelled throughout Uganda and Kenya. It was at the start of the trip that a man had come along side and was trying to influence where I would go and who I would spend time with. This man claimed to be a pastor with many contacts, but I was getting a witness in my spirit that he was not what he claimed to be. Even one day he followed me in to an ATM booth where I had gone to lift some money. He demanded that I lift far more money than I was doing. I ordered him out. It was this that showed me that he was money orientated. More and more I was discerning there was a spirit in this man, and it was not the Spirit of God. More and more I was sensing evil coming across. I just could not put my finger on it, but I just knew.

After discussing it with Pastor Godfrey we prayed again for the protection of the Blood and entrusted ourselves into the Lord's keeping. That was the only thing and the very best thing I could do. This 'false pastor' wished to go with us to Kenya but I was feeling very uneasy in my spirit and I was very emphatic this should not happen. A few days earlier I had spoken with my trusted friend, Pastor Antony, and expressed my worries. He arranged for his brother to meet us and move us to where we would be ministering. When we arrived in Kenya the 'false pastor' appeared and he had two other friends arrive also claiming to be pastors. They were most insistent I would go in a car with them, but we firmly refused. The trio were anything but happy with me. They then changed tactic and suggested that it was too far to travel late in the evening so they had a hotel we would all stay in and next morning I could travel on. By this time, I was getting a little scared and was praying for our friend's brother to come and rescue us. God answered prayer because I saw this tall and well-built man striding along towards us. I ran down to meet him just knowing he was our man and sure enough he was. When he was quickly filled in on the goings on, he took control and asked the men to leave. Then came the punch line: "We have no money. Can you pay for us to stay in an hotel and buy us tickets to fly back to Uganda?"

Looking back, I can laugh at the audacity of them, but it was very unsettling at the time. We knew then they were dangerous and false prophets. Thank God for the gift of discernment. All went well from then on in Kenya and souls were saved at each crusade. It came time then to head back to Uganda to finish the mission work there. Pastor Godfrey and I did not fly back; we always move around the cheapest way to conserve the finances. We got a taxi to take us the long journey back.

The taxis are not like what we have in the western world. They are sixteen-seater vehicles which are always vastly over-crowed transporting as many as can get in and physically sitting half on the next person's knee. Many times, the vehicle would be moving along the road at a great speed while passengers, with their feet on the running board, holding on to the roof-rack whilst hanging out through the window. No health and safety there and I doubt if any of the taxis would pass our MOT's here in the UK.

I arrived about eight or nine hours later to where I was staying on the outskirts of Kampala and was glad to see a clean bed for the night. During the night I heard someone in around and they tried to open my door. It did not annoy me unduly as I knew I had locked it but the next morning Pastor Godfrey arrived and said we were moving to another area for the weekend. This was not on the schedule, but I knew I had a close and trusted confidante in this young man, so I threw a few things into a bag quickly as he had arranged for a car to come and collect us to take us to a taxi bay.

We travelled another four-and-a-half-hour journey to a village and got somewhere to sleep. The next day we visited a school and a pastor's home. Another pastor came to see me, and I was invited to preach for him at his church the next morning. There was to be two services. The first commencing at 8:00 a.m. until 10:30 a.m. and the second from 10:30 a.m. to approximately 2:00 p.m. That was fine I got prepared for that and was looking forward to fellowshipping there. My calm and peaceful state of mind was soon to get a rude shaking before too long.

Just as I was thinking of retiring for the night Pastor Godfrey said he had something to share with me. I knew by his demeanour it was serious so I got ready to listen carefully, but nothing could have prepared me for what was coming. With head bowed and elbows resting on his knees he said, "Mummy, I have had to move you quickly well away from Kampala for your own safety." I laughed slightly, then I realised he was not joking but was deadly serious.

The 'false pastor' who was following me from the beginning had issued threats against me because I would not give him money. Pastor Godfrey had spoken with someone for advice and that was how I come to be where I was for the weekend. After church on the Sunday we would go to a senior pastor's home and there the head of Ugandan security would ring and speak with me regarding the matter. You may guess I did not sleep much that night.

Sunday morning, I was up around 6:00 a.m. but my mind was in turmoil. When we went out to get on the motorbikes to travel for the first service, I shared with Pastor Godfrey the night I had and how I felt I could not preach. He had been praying and I knew that unless the Holy Spirit took complete control there was not going to be any preaching. This is how I should always be on entering a pulpit but that morning I was praying for God to take my mind and my thoughts captive for the things He would have me say. Praise God we had a mighty time, and many were saved at both services. All glory to our God and King.

After church we walked to the other pastor's home and enjoyed fellowship together. Then the phone call took place. The captain advised that I should not travel that evening as we had planned but very early the next morning and go straight to security head office in Kampala. There I would be briefed and told what to do.

Suffice to say here, I was under a death threat. The trio of men did not have churches and they were all working together to con money out of white people like me who they saw as easy prey. In fact, about a week or fortnight before I arrived, they had tried the same move with another white person and when they did not get the money that person was killed. It was a real threat and their priority they said was to "keep me safe and when the time came get me to the airport and on my flight safe and well out of their country."

I stayed the day there and at an appointed time two cars, one with the captain plus one of his team, the other with

Pastor Godfrey and I left and we travelled to go and collect my things and be moved to a safe place. Was I not glad I had the captain and his team because it proved very difficult and without their physical intervention, I might not be writing this today? I was scared! I was so frightened! The false pastor was waiting for me to collect my things and tried to prevent me unless I would hand over a very large sum of money. After threatening, abusive words, and trying to intimidate me into subjection by going to call the police, my security men stepped forward and revealed to him that they were special police. He did not believe them, but they showed their security ID and took complete control from that point.

Thanks to the captain and his colleague I collected my belongings, the 'false pastor' was taken in their car, and Pastor Godfrey and I were moved to another safe place – a hotel with security outside. I was extremely shaken and just could not go to bed. It had only hit me that this threat was for real and I was in actual danger. Then I called to memory the lovely promise in scripture Psalm 91:4, *"He shall cover thee with his feathers, and under his wings shalt thou trust: his truth shall be thy shield and buckler."*

True to their word security looked after me right through even arranging my check-in and departure from the airport to fly out home. When I entered the airport, I was met and my cases were taken and a white sticker put on them which read, 'airport security checked'. A gentleman took me straight to get my ticket at the check-in desk. I was left in a 'safe place' until someone took me to the plane. Though the flight was fully booked I was the only one seated in my row right across the plane. Thank God for these born-again men whom He brought along into my life. These Divine connections yet again meant I was out, and on my way home safe. Every time since then that I visit Africa, Pastor Godfrey is always by my side protecting me and watching out for all eventualities that might occur. I count myself privileged yet I am most humbled to call the Captain my friend and brother in the Lord.

If God had not given me the spirit of discernment, I would not have sensed there was a problem with the 'false pastor' and fallen into his trap. In Kenya I might have got into the car with 'three false pastors' thinking I should be fine in their company. Who knows where they would have taken me or what they might have done. I know now they had only evil intentions. There is much more to this story that I cannot share for security reasons, but I continually thank God for protecting Pastor Godfrey and myself and giving Pastor Godfrey the word of knowledge to get me moved away quickly on that Friday morning.

To conclude on 1John 4:1, *"Beloved, believe not every spirit, but try the spirits whether they are of God: because many false prophets (teachers and preachers) are gone out into the world."*

I am not to be easily taken in or easily led is what John is saying. And he is saying that to you also. He says to test, check and search the scriptures. Look out for false preacher and those who are lying, are manipulative and self-seeking.

I note here the words, "gone out into the world". 'Gone out' suggests to me that they have one aim and one purpose and that is to deceive. I note also the word 'many'. It is not one or two. It is not a few but they are many. We see this up and down our land today. They are filling the pulpits, the 'God and religious channels' on the television to name but a few. Begging for money and if you pay a little you will be blessed a little but if you pay more you will be blessed more. Many of these men and woman are false preachers and are going to hell themselves and taking their congregation and listeners with them. What an indictment! How will they answer before God and what will they say to the people who will be in hell because of them?

King Solomon, who is considered the wisest king ever to live, said in Proverbs 14:15, "*The simple believeth every word: but the prudent man looketh well to his going.*"

You and I need to have a discerning spirit which only God can give us. However, we always have the bible with us, and we can measure what we hear against the yardstick of scripture. If it measures short or is not at all, you and I must cast it away from us as evil and the one who speaks the lies as wolves in sheep's clothing. I close this chapter with the words from the Book of Galatians 6:7-8, "*Be not deceived; God is not mocked: for whatsoever a man soweth, that shall he also reap. For he that soweth to his flesh shall of the flesh reap corruption; but he that soweth to the Spirit shall of the Spirit reap life everlasting.*"

Let God's Word be the final say. I can say I was truly tried test and protected by Almighty God. All glory to His matchless name.

A Cave, A Prison, A Grave

Whether in downtown or villages in the African countries I have visited, life for the average person is much the same. Let me share with you just a little of what I experienced as I was driven around.

Everything looks very old and dirty regardless of what it is. The homes, the buildings, the shops, the cars, and the people all look poor and neglected. I had to try and get my head around the driving in both city or town. It just begs belief as it is total madness and even though they are third world countries vehicles are many on the roads. I refer to the road as African massage roads as they are so poor and full of large potholes that if you were to drive into one, as we did one day, you just burst the tyre at best or destroy the wheel or even break a spring.

The trucks have only a hint of paint and it would appear to me that one is permitted to scrape the remaining paint off as they pass if the metal is left behind. Minibuses are without bumpers and cars which are battered have windows held in by string or duct tape. The doors may not even close completely, but as long as the engine works and the wheels go around, the vehicles are deemed worthy to be on the road. I have even seen chewing gum used to hold a window from falling or to hold an inside mirror in place. It appears to me that indicators are an optional extra and tail-light are often poor or non-existent even on police vehicles. When an accident occurs, it is a major incident with often a serious loss of life.

No health and safety standards to be met there and certainly no MOT to be passed and certificate issued to confirm the vehicle is road worthy and legal. There are donkey and carts, bicycles and motorbikes everywhere and each one drives around as though they are the only ones should be on the road. The buses have people hanging out the windows tightly clutching their sacks and baskets with hens tied to the door posts or in the boot and large sacks transported on the roof racks. There are trucks full of cattle and then a crowd of people on the very top hanging on for dear life to the top frame; anything to make their journey easier and quicker. Many times, the cyclists are to be seen holding on to the back of trucks to gain extra speed and to save on pedal power.

The pedestrians dice with death as they dash across the five lane traffic in what should only be a two lane intersection. Even in the city of Kampala I witnessed six lanes of traffic in what should have been a four-lane intersection. Even on our side of the road we negotiated against two lanes of vehicles coming against the traffic. Better still, the police were standing back watching but doing absolutely nothing about it. When I asked why I was told that it was the norm and the police only get involved if there is a serious accident. Traffic signals are optional and stop signs are only a suggestion as everyone makes up their own rules on where and when to drive. The right of way comes down to who is the bravest. I would venture to say that to have a driving license is one thing but to be able to drive on the roads one would not need to be of a nervous disposition. The SAS motto of "*Who dares wins*" would be very applicable.

The sides of the streets are lined with small kiosks selling everything imaginable from phone top-up cards, clothes, fruit and vegetables, second-hand clothes and shoes, hens, and raw meat, and then a host of fresh food being sold to eat on the move. The food is cooked over charcoal on the roadside and there is no running water, but water brought over in jerry cans. The flies seemed to do best as they got the first taste and then the customers buy after that. No small wonder there is so much sickness among the people.

My very first trip to Africa which took me to Uganda, I did indeed question my sanity a few times, but I knew beyond any shadow of doubt God had called me and placed me there to serve Him. This gave me the calm assurance that despite a great culture shock I would be able to cope because God had, and still does, promise His grace and mercy for each new day. I could and would do all things through Christ who would strengthen me. But what was God teaching me? What lessons were there for me to learn? I knew that with every new experience and situation God had a purpose and it was up to me to take time to listen and learn at His feet. Then I could action what I learned.

The first thing I noticed was that all these 'average' people were in a cave that was not always of their own making. They were born into poverty and this cave of poverty they could either remain in or take action to escape the cave. I had once been in a cave of sickness following my stroke but with God's help I chose to leave that cave. There are many caves you and I can run into and hide from the world; the cave of depression, the cave of hurt from a brother or sister, the cave of sickness and disease, the cave of fear, the cave of meagre supplies, the cave of hiding from God. Each one of us will run and hide in a cave at some time in our life and only you know what cave you are dwelling in. When trials come that is when you and I are prone to 'cave in' and dwell there in the dark cave.

One thing I was to learn quickly was that a cave can quickly become a prison. A prison of our own making that we cannot escape from because we choose to remain rather than begin to praise and get raised to freedom. The longer you and I dwell in the cave the more of a prison it becomes. It gets to be a place where we find a false sense of security and we are loath to even take a peep outside just in case we make matters worse. The cave you and I have run into becomes a prison but eventually that prison becomes a grave.

That is what it is like for so many of the families in Africa. They accept their fate; they cave in and never try to do anything but to exist from day to day and most probably they will die before or in middle age. The next generation will repeat the cycle and on and on it goes. I am not blaming them but rather use their plight to give you an everyday illustration of a cave becoming a prison becoming a grave.

Let us take a read in the scriptures and see what we can learn.

> *"David therefore departed thence, and escaped to the cave Adullam: and when his brethren and all his father's house heard it, they went down thither to him. And every one that was in distress, and every one that was in debt, and every one that was discontented, gathered themselves unto him; and he became a captain over them: and there were with him about four hundred men. And David went thence to Mizpeh of Moab: and he said unto the king of Moab, Let my father and my mother, I pray thee, come forth, and be with you, till I know what God will do for me. And he brought them before the king of Moab: and they dwelt with him all the while that David was in the hold."* 1Samuel 22:1-4

"Hear my cry, O God; attend unto my prayer. From the end of the earth will I cry unto thee, when my heart is overwhelmed: lead me to the rock that is higher than I."
Psalm 61:1-2

Listen to what David said in those verses. Do you ever feel overwhelmed by life? We all do from time to time! This text finds David in one of those times. He is in a dark, damp, dreary, depressing cave. He has experienced the loss of everything and everyone he leaned on in his life. He is alone, defeated and discouraged. David is in one of the cave experiences of life.

What David did not see at the time, but soon came to understand, was the fact that God was behind it all and in control of it all. David did not know it at the time, but God was going to use his time in the cave to help David grow stronger in the Lord. The day would soon come when David would emerge from that cave far stronger in the Lord than he was when he entered that time in his life.

There are times when we too find ourselves in one of life's cave experiences. We think all of our help and strength is gone. We feel alone, discouraged and deserted. Ever been there? Sure you have. In fact, some of you reading this are there right now! Well, like David, when we are dwelling in one of the caves of life, we often fail to see the hand of God in what we are facing. But, I would remind you today that just as surely as God is behind all the blessings of life; He is behind all the burdens as well.

"I form the light, and create darkness: I make peace, and create evil: I the LORD do all these things."
Isaiah 45:7

"The steps of a good man are ordered by the LORD: and he delighteth in his way." Psalm 37:23

"For whom he did foreknow, he also did predestinate to be conformed to the image of his Son, that he might be the firstborn among many brethren." Romans 8:29

This passage contains some blessings that you and I need to consider today. Here, we can learn something about the cave experiences of life and how we can come out of them and out stronger than we entered them. I want to take this episode from the life of David and look at climbing out of or leaving our cave. Notice the blessings that are contained in this passage.

The Realities of the Cave - verse 1

A. The Reality of Sorrow — David has been brought to the absolute bottom of life! He is hurting, he is broken, and he is defeated. The Crown Prince of Israel is living in a cave! He does not rest his head on a sumptuous bed in the palace, but on the unyielding rocks of a cave! He no longer sleeps in the bed of the princes, but he seeks rest in the damp darkness of a forsaken cave. He does not find comfort in the house of a friend, but he fights loneliness in a deserted, dirty cave. Psalm 142 was written during this period of time.

There are times like that ordained for each of us as well. I should not expect to get through this life untouched and unaffected by hardship and sorrow and neither should you. In fact, the Bible is perfectly clear about this matter, Job 14:1, *"Man that is born of a woman is of few days, and full of trouble."*; in John 16:33 Jesus says; *"These things I have spoken unto you, that in me ye might have peace. In the world ye shall have tribulation: but be of good cheer; I have overcome the world."*

Just as they were for David, sorrows are part of our earthly experience. Thank God for a home where they cannot follow us. Revelation 21:4, *"And God shall wipe away all tears from their eyes; and there shall be no more death, neither sorrow, nor crying, neither shall there be any more pain: for the former things are passed away."* Hallelujah! What a promise to stand on.

B. The Reality of Suffering — God allowed David to come to this cave so that David might learn not to lean on the props of family, friends, finances, fame, the flesh or the future. David was taught, through his sufferings, to wholly lean upon the Lord. You see, God was not trying to destroy David. He was not trying to discipline David. God was attempting to develop David into the man of God the Lord wanted him to become.

The same is true in your life and in mine. To teach us to look to Him alone, the Lord uses the hardships of life to develop us. God does not do this to break us; He does it to build us. However, times of breaking up and tearing down often come before the times of building up! (Hebrews 12:5-13) As hard as it may be to understand and bear, God uses the times of affliction, suffering and pain in your life and mine to train us to become more like His darling Son Jesus.

C. The Reality of Separation - David has been cut off from his family, his friends and his followers. He is in a place that prevents fellowship with others. This could have easily been his prison and indeed it was for some time but here David was brought to the place where he had nothing and no one but the Lord God. That cave was a place of separation – a prison.

I often find myself in the caves as well, don't you too? God will bring us to the place where we are alone with Him and shut off from the rest of the world. I fear those times, but they often precede the times of God's greatest blessings in my life as long as I am prepared to be obedient and learn. David was alone in the cave. Jacob too, was alone in his tent. Elijah also was alone by the brook. Job may as well have been alone surrounded by his so-called friends. Moses was alone on the backside of the mountain. Jesus was alone in the agony of Gethsemane and Calvary. Each of these experienced their greatest triumph after that time of being shut up and shut off by the Lord. You see, there are lessons that are learned in the dark that cannot be learned in the light. There are truths that can only be understood by those who are cut off and shut up with the Lord. That is only if you and I are to use our experience and time in the cave wisely.

In reality, the cave times of life can be a blessed time of instruction and growth. You see, I may not like it, and I may not understand it, but when the Lord has brought me to a place where I have no one and nothing but Him, He has done me a tremendous favour. Why? He is more than sufficient; He is more than enough; and He will never leave me.

> *"Let your conversation be without covetousness; and be content with such things as ye have: for he hath said, I will never leave thee, nor forsake thee."* Hebrews 13:5

> *"God is our refuge and strength, a very present help in trouble."* Psalm 46:1

The Revelations of the Cave - verse 1-4

A. The Revelation of His Call — As David's props began to be taken away, one after the other, he probably began to doubt the promises that God had made to him so long ago. But, after a while, people began to show up at David's cave. First, his family came; then the defeated and downtrodden men of Israel began to show up. David's family came out of fear of Saul; the rest came because they believed David was God's man for the future. There is a big difference in the two groups of people. One lot of people can build the cave dweller up, but the other group can help to turn the cave to a prison which eventually will become a grave. It is still the same today for you and for me. We will have the negative soothsayers and we will also have the child of God who is on fire and in touch with God. Who should we give ear to? God does use people to bring us a message or/and to bless us.

Why do I say that the cave can become our grave? Take Lazarus; he was in a cave bound with grave clothes because as far as the world was concerned, he was dead. A cave is where the dead were buried. Life only came into the cave when Christ spoke and called Lazarus to come forth. When Christ is present life is in abundance. Lazarus was released from his grave clothes and walked forth alive and well. A cave is where we find dead bodies – remains. But where Jesus is there is life. Darkness cannot exist when the Light of the world, Jesus Christ the Son of God, is present.

They all cast in their lot with David. God used this motley group of people to show David that He still had a plan for his life.

I don't know how God will do it, but somehow, while you and I are in our cave, He will come to where we are and confirm His faithfulness and His promises to us. God will use our cave as a banner to write His love over our life. Elijah had his ravens; Moses had his burning bush; Jesus had His empty tomb, (and we will come back to this point later). God has a way of showing us that it will be all right.

B. The Revelation of His Character — When his family and the malcontents of Israel showed up, it probably added to David's burden at first. Psalm 57, which was also written during that time, expresses that thought in verse 4; *"My soul is among lions: and I lie even among them that are set on fire, even the sons of men, whose teeth are spears and arrows, and their tongue a sharp sword."*

But David rose to the challenge and the truth of his character was revealed in what he did during those times. He took measures to care for his elderly parents and he rose up and led his men. In other words, instead of breaking under the pressures of the moment, David's heart was revealed. The leader rose to the challenge and led! But it took pain and problems to squeeze that out of him!

Just as it did in the life of David, suffering and pain will reveal exactly what we have in our hearts as well. Take Job for example. He suffered! Satan said to God, *"put forth thine hand now, and touch all that he hath, and he will curse thee to thy face."* So, satan attacked Job and what happened? Job did not get angry with the Lord; he just shouted in the devil's face and got sweeter, Job 1:20-21, *"Then Job arose, and rent his mantle, and shaved his head, and fell down upon the ground, and worshipped, And said, Naked came I out of my mother's womb, and naked shall I return thither: the LORD gave, and the LORD hath taken away; blessed be the name of the LORD."*

What comes out of you and me when the pressure is applied? Do you get bitter and angry when trouble comes or, do you and I display integrity and keep on praising the Lord; knowing that He is in control and will work all things out for His glory? Suffering will expose our heart like few other things can.

C. The Revelation of His Commitment — In spite of what the circumstances said about David and his situation, David held on to the promises of God. Psalm 57 is what I will call one of David's cave psalms.

> *"Be merciful unto me, O God, be merciful unto me: for my soul trusteth in thee: yea, in the shadow of thy wings will I make my refuge, until these calamities be overpast. I will cry unto God most high; unto God that performeth all things for me. He shall send from heaven, and save me from the reproach of him that would swallow me up. Selah. God shall send forth his mercy and his truth. My soul is among lions: and I lie even among them that are set on fire, even the sons of men, whose teeth are spears and arrows, and their tongue a sharp sword. Be thou exalted, O God, above the heavens; let thy glory be above all the earth. They have prepared a net for my steps; my soul is bowed down: they have digged a pit before me, into the midst whereof they are fallen themselves. Selah. My heart is fixed, O God, my heart is fixed: I will sing and give praise. Awake up, my glory; awake, psaltery and harp: I myself will awake early. I will praise thee, O Lord, among the people: I will sing unto thee among the nations. For thy mercy is great unto the heavens, and thy truth unto the clouds. Be thou exalted, O God, above the heavens: let thy glory be above all the earth."*
> Psalm 57:1-11

David knew where to go to find refuge in the times of trouble. He did not give up, even when most others would have. He held on to the Lord and the promises of God. He knew that God would come through in His time!

How good and well it would be that you and I could display that kind of commitment in our own hearts and lives.

When the pressure is on, don't turn on the Lord but remain committed to Him! He knows what He is doing, and He will not fail you and He will not fail me. With this a fact then, don't you fail Him Eileen. Nothing demonstrates our level of commitment to God than our continued obedience and faithful service, even when you and I are in one of the caves of life.

The Refreshments of the Cave - verse 2

Caves make for hard living, but they are not altogether bad! There are some refreshing discoveries to be made in the caves of life.

A. The Refreshment of His Family — David's family comes to him in that cave. Here are people who used to doubt David. His own father ignored him, 1 Samuel 16:11, "*And Samuel said unto Jesse, Are here all thy children? And he said, There remaineth yet the youngest, and, behold, he keepeth the sheep. And Samuel said unto Jesse, Send and fetch him: for we will not sit down till he come hither.*" His oldest brother Eliab publicly rebuked David and criticized him, 1Samuel 17:28 "*And Eliab his eldest brother heard when he spake unto the men; and Eliab's anger was kindled against David, and he said, Why camest thou down hither? and with whom hast thou left those few sheep in the wilderness? I know thy pride, and the naughtiness of thine heart; for thou art come down that thou mightest see the battle.*"

Now, they see in the man before them God's man and God's choice for king. The one they formerly would have passed over is the one they turn to for help. It seems that the caves of life have the potential to bring out our best. Remember the prophet Samuel had anointed David as the future king under the direction of God

As an evangelist/pastor, I have seen many people suffer horrible things. I am always fascinated by how people respond to the pain they are called upon to bear. I have seen some crumple under the load. They have literally fallen apart and sunk down into the pit of self-pity. Equally, there have been others who, despite the great load of suffering they were forced to carry, rose to the challenge and tapped into a source of strength they did not know they possessed. They were changed by their experience and still others were changed by watching them go through it. You see, it is not the storms you weather that define you; it is the way that you weather the storms. Did you get that?

In 2010, I watched a young man die. He had gotten sick very suddenly and he was on a life support machine. The doctors told his family that nothing more could be done for him. His poor dear wife sat beside his bed and she would talk to him. This went on for two weeks. Then, one day the decision was made to turn the machine off. His wife leaned over, kissed his cheek, and said, "It's all right. You can go on now. I'll miss you, I have loved you dearly." She sat back down and within just a few minutes that precious man was gone. His wife rose to the challenge that night! She won a newfound respect in the eyes of all who saw her enter her cave and pass through it with grace and dignity.

B. The Refreshment of His Followers — These men who gathered themselves around David were there because they were fed up with Saul. The distressed came to David. This word used in Hebrew means 'to be under stress and under pressure.' We are also told that those who were in debt came. This speaks of those who 'could not pay their bills.' The discontented also came. This word refers to those who are 'bitter and who have been mistreated.' Here was a group of hundreds of people who have suffered under the tyranny and taxation of Saul and they are fed up. They find themselves in a dark place and do not know what to do. They are looking for leadership. They go to David because they believe that he is God's man for Israel.

I am sure that David could not see in his life what they saw. At that time, David could only feel defeat and discouragement. While David could only see the cave he was in; those who came to him could see the crown. They gathered themselves around him and believed in him, even when he was down. David was encouraged and was determined not to allow his cave which had been a prison to become his grave.

Thank God for the encouragers of life. Thank God for those people who can see potential in my life and in yours, when we can see nothing good in ourselves. Barnabas was that kind of a friend to Mark, Acts 15:35-41. Apparently, it had a lasting effect on the young man's life and ministry because Paul writes to Timothy in 2Timothy 4:11, "*...Take Mark, and bring him with thee: for he is profitable to me for the ministry.*"

God has a way of putting people around each one of us who can serve as encouragers in our lives! I praise the Lord for everyone who has looked at my life and seen potential there that I could not recognize. What an encouragement they have been to me.

It is worthy of note here to state there is a great need for this kind of ministry in the church today. There is always someone who stands ready to criticize and cut down; but there are very few who will come along side during the hard times of our life and lift us up. Maybe God is calling you into that kind of ministry for His glory. It is profitable to the Lord's work to be an encourager

C. The Refreshment of His Focus — Going through the pain of seeing all his props taken away was a painful experience for David. Having to flee from the palace to hide in a cave was humbling as well. However, in that humble hide away, God began the process of transforming David into a great king. God took that rough band of men and, working through David, transformed them into *"David's Mighty Men."* These men, and their exploits, are named in 2Samuel 23. Because God sent these men to David in the cave, David was able to get his mind of his problems and focus his attention on leading them and training them to be a fighting force. It was a humble beginning, but David was focused and soon he would walk out of that cave and accept the crown. The cave was where he learned to be brave. The prison was opened up to freedom, and death could not occur where God was allowed to operate.

If there is any one benefit of the cave that stands out, it is the fact that caves have the ability to focus our priorities. When I go into a cave experience, I soon learn what is important and what is trivial. The caves of life help me to focus like nothing else can do.

Peter, one of the disciples of the inner circle, was all over the place; blowing hot and cold, before he entered his cave experience and denied Christ. But when he came out of that cave he was focused and sharp for the Lord. That is what the cave will do for you. It will fasten your focus onto that which is most important: finding and doing the will of the Lord. Sometimes, I think that is why the Lord allows us to enter caves. But, a cave can either make us brave or become our grave.

In Jonah chapter one, we read how Jonah is running from God, but a few days in a cave helps to focus his attention and he begins to run with God. His cave was in the belly of the great fish. If the cave can do that, then it cannot be all bad.

David entered his cave a broken and defeated man. He could have remained there in his prison and with a wrong mindset and upon death the cave would become his grave, but not so; he emerged as the captain of an army of mighty men. He went in running from a crazy king. He came out reaching out to take the crown. The cave refined David's life and helped to prepare him for the tasks that lay ahead. He grew because in the cave he submitted to the will of God. He became brave!

What about you? Are your cave experiences blessings to your life, or are they burdens that seem too heavy to carry? If you need some help dealing with a cave experience in your life, you will find the help you need in the presence of the Lord. Go to Him and get what you need right now. We can choose to live in the fear of the past or move forward in faith into our potential of the future. You and I can't do this on or in our own strength but with and through Christ we surely can.

I wish to close this chapter by going back to the point I made earlier regarding Christ in the cave. When Christ was crucified and buried His body was wrapped in grave clothes and laid in a borrowed tomb/cave with a large stone rolled across to secure it. But, unlike all others gone before, Christ did not remain in the tomb, but He had power over death hell and the grave and arose on the third day. He had in His hand the keys of death hell and the grave. Jesus Christ said Himself regarding His own life; "I have power to lay it down and I have power to take it up again." Blessed be the name of the Lord.

This same Jesus Christ can give you and me the power to move out of our cave so we may live to serve Him every day of our life. Life is easy when you are up on the mountain. You have got peace of mind. But remember the God of the mountain is still God in the valley and still God in the cave you are in. I love the hymn and the words are precious and so true.

Tears often fall on my face in sorrow
As I walk on through the long lonely night
Often I cry but it seems no one hears me
But then through the shadows I can see the dawning of light.

Chorus
Oh soon this old life with all of its trials
Will be left behind there's a new day a dawning
The shadow of sin will vanish forever
He's promised me there's going to be
Joy in the Morning

Tears cannot stain the pathways of glory
No broken hearts we'll find up there
Beyond that sky my mansion's awaiting
By the light of the morning we'll sing the songs
Of sweet victory

So hold on my child, joy comes in the morning
Weeping only last for the night
Hold on my child joy comes in the morning
The darkest hour means dawn is just in sight
Oh yes the darkest hour means dawn is just in sight.

If you've knelt beside the rubble
of an aching broken heart
When the things you gave your life to fell apart.
You're not the first to be acquainted
with sorrow, grief or pain
But the Master promised sunshine after rain.

Chorus
Hold on my child joy comes in the morning
Weeping only last for the night
Hold on my child Joy comes in the morning
The darkest hour means dawn is just in sight

To invest your seeds of trust in God
in mountains you can't move
You have risked your life on things you cannot prove
But to give the things you cannot keep
for what you cannot lose
Now, that's the way to find the joy God has for you

Lyrics by: Bill Gaither

Remember; if you complain you remain but if you praise you get raised, Child of God, rise up today and keep on praising the Lord.

What does the Future Hold?

Man, Church and Nations

There is no doubting that there are perplexities of nations. There is no doubting that the heavens and the earth are being shaken up. There is no doubting that the church, by and large, is not fit for purpose and the 'Church' is very lukewarm and at sleep. There is no doubting that man has got arrogant, prideful, self-seeking, and lovers of self rather than lovers of God. In fact, society today is so fallen in moral behaviour and the governments and members so corrupt that one could be forgiven to think there was no way back and just throw the hands up in utter despair.

Let us look at a few of the problems and try and find solutions?

Preachers are called to feed the flock NOT fleece the flock!

It is important to me that I always challenge the participants of a conference with a message of urgency and this should be very important to every preacher. Preaching the Gospel is not a passive ministry. An 'un-preached' Gospel is no Gospel at all. There has never been a revival without aggressive evangelism. Each generation has only their lifetime to reach their generation and time is running out.

Away with all this prosperity preaching! If you give "x" amount God will bless you with a new car, more finance, or something else is offered more tantalising. Preachers living in mansion houses dripping in gold and some even have private jets. Friend this sort of preaching is from the pit of hell. Satan is subtle and deceiving as he did in the Garden of Eden and the scripture is being twisted with no call to repentance and a forsaking of sins. That is not what I read in my Bible.

You may be thinking this is a strange study but in recent days I have become very aware of churches who have false prophets in their pulpits and yet others who have people in position that have very clearly a Jezebel spirit within them and the preacher is not prepared to act or deal with the matter.

This is a very serious matter and a minister or pastor who refuses to face up to the problem and have it eradicated immediately will face serious consequences both in his congregation but ultimately from God Himself. God will not tolerate this, and the Holy Spirit cannot operate. It will not be long until the word *'Ichabod'* (the glory of the Lord has departed. 1Samuel 2:21) is seen over the church. Do not be deceived God is not mocked. Let us consider what the Word of God says on this matter

Jesus warned us to watch out for wolves in sheep's clothing. Clearly this means identifying people who claim to be Christians but inwardly are ravening wolves. So, are there any New Testament examples of people who were exposed as wolves in sheep's clothing? Some come to my mind.

Paul warns us, too. He says that in the last days perilous times shall come. Do we all agree that we are in the last days? Isn't this important to recognize.

"Now we beseech you, brethren, by the coming of our Lord Jesus Christ, and by our gathering together unto him, That ye be not soon shaken in mind, or be troubled, neither by spirit, nor by word, nor by letter as from us, as that the day of Christ is at hand. Let no man deceive you by any means: for that day shall not come, except there come a falling away first, and that man of sin be revealed, the son of perdition; Who opposeth and exalteth himself above all that is called God, or that is worshipped; so that he as God sitteth in the temple of God, shewing himself that he is God. Remember ye not, that, when I was yet with you, I told you these things? And now ye know what withholdeth that he might be revealed in his time. For the mystery of iniquity doth already work: only he who now letteth will let, until he be taken out of the way." 2Thessalonians 2:1-7

Paul also writes:
"Holding faith, and a good conscience; which some having put away concerning faith have made shipwreck: Of whom is Hymenaeus and Alexander; whom I have delivered unto Satan, that they may learn not to blaspheme." 1 Timothy 1:19-20

Would you consider them wolves in sheep's clothing or just backsliders? I strongly believe they are wolves in sheep's clothing, false teachers and false prophets.

Paul said that Demas had forsaken him, having loved this present world and departed for Thessalonica (2Timothy 4:10). Would that be a wolf, or simply a backslider?

What about the people that joined in the agape feasts that Jude refers to?

"For there are certain men crept in unawares, who were before of old ordained to this condemnation, ungodly men, turning the grace of our God into lasciviousness, and denying the only Lord God, and our Lord Jesus Christ....Likewise also these filthy dreamers defile the flesh, despise dominion, and speak evil of dignities.... But these speak evil of those things which they know not: but what they know naturally, as brute beasts, in those things they corrupt themselves. Woe unto them! for they have gone in the way of Cain, and ran greedily after the error of Balaam for reward, and perished in the gainsaying of Core. These are spots in your feasts of charity, when they feast with you, feeding themselves without fear: clouds they are without water, carried about of winds; trees whose fruit withereth, without fruit, twice dead, plucked up by the roots; Raging waves of the sea, foaming out their own shame; wandering stars, to whom is reserved the blackness of darkness for ever." Jude 4, 8, 10-13

Those are harsh words regarding people who are calling themselves Christians and are/was in their fellowship. Paul believed that had to be said, the issue had to be dealt with and there could be no compromising. What stark warnings for us who are living in these very last days mentioned. I am no Paul, but I am a teacher and a preacher so therefore I must speak up and speak out. Wake up! Do you hear me? Wake up, get up, and action up. Don't cover up for someone in your church. Challenge them and if they refuse to acknowledge God's warning then kick them out. You must not allow their spirit to permeate the church and to mislead the congregation.

This is spiritual discernment and I believe every serious follower of Christ should have it. So let me share some thoughts to help understand what clues will demonstrate a wolf in sheep's clothing...

One of the clear signs, or most obvious, is a wolf will get you thinking temporal. The simplest example I can give is, "Give me money for this cloth I've soaked in a blessing and your financial troubles will be healed or your marriage or your family relations or your career advancement or your vehicle situation. How often have we listened to this on the television as well as been subjected to it for real? Another one often spoken is, "for a financial gift of … God will move in your situation and…" It just makes me so sick; but how do you think God views these people and their shenanigans? No small wonder that we have so many very rich TV evangelists. Everything from God is free. All we have to do is go before Him with clean hands and a pure heart.

Jesus was always eternally minded, and a true shepherd of the Lord will be also, overall anyway, concerned about your eternal state. Good popular leaders of the past, even if we may disagree on some theological points, always pointed to our eternal future while most leaders of popularity today point to our temporal existence, lording over God's people and making a great comfort of living in the here and now while the majority of those who give them money have little in the way of comfort and is why they can extort them because of the hope of a better temporal outcome.

Jesus taught us if we are poor consider ourselves rich and if rich consider ourselves poor. We have an eternal future beyond our imagination. As we grow in Jesus, we all get smarter. We can improve are condition if we focus on Jesus and not some swindler making promises and speaking things that do not come true.

There are many answers to this question.

It's the subtle snakes that are difficult. But Jesus said to be as wise as serpents but harmless as doves. Understanding the wiles of the devil is something we are called to do. Jesus warned of deception in Matthew 24 more than all other warnings concerning His coming and the end of the age. Its real easy to spot an out-right false prophet as against one who is in error.

The key to this type of person is found when you go to, and then correct the erring member if they flat out won't hear and repent then my friend... they are as false as it is possible to be. But anyone who is in error that person will hear and repent willingly.

Now, as far as teachers goes the one who is leading the flock should have been long tested and tried and should never have been a novice. What do I mean by that? They should not be doing so just because they felt led. They need to be taught and mature before they can lead others. He needs to be well engrained in the Holy Scriptures alone. Well learned and a good example in Christ.

Sad to say, the pulpits are full of people like this, immature, misguided, or in it for a living. Folks, we have got serious issues. Most of them are false, but worse, the people cannot discern them. They actually love and adore what these men and women of Jezebel teach.

What about you? Are you one of these people, either a false leader or a member of the congregation who condone what is going on? It is a disgrace but come and experience God's grace. Today, God is saying repent. Preacher, each weekend and at every opportunity given you, as you go to your church and go into the pulpit preach the whole counsel of God and do not twist the scriptures for your own benefit. When men fail you God will never fail.

1. Watch out.

"Beware of false prophets, who come to you in sheep's clothing but inwardly are ravenous wolves."
Matthew 7:15

God reminds us in His Word to 'watch out,' 'beware,' to stay awake. He knows and understands how difficult it can be to fight this spiritual battle. Some days we get weary, or we get so busy and distracted, we're not watching anymore for ways we might get tripped up. But he tells us, *"Watch ye, stand fast in the faith, quit you like men, be strong."* 1 Corinthians 16:13

God desires the best for us and knows how important it is for us to live aware. He freely gives us his strength and protection to stand strong each day, He will never leave us defenceless on our own.

2. Know the real and you'll know the fake too.

"Ye shall know them by their fruits..." Matthew 7:16

God's Word is clear, it says they'll be known by their fruits. Not by how much money they have. Not by how many followers they have. Not by how many books they have written or the great things they have done. They'll be known by what fruit exists in their lives. Is there love, joy, peace, patience, kindness, goodness, gentleness, faithfulness, and self-control? Are they sharing the gospel of Christ, and pointing others to the forgiveness and freedom that He alone can bring? What do they say about who Jesus is? What do they believe about the authority of God's Word?

We may have to look more closely than what is on the outside. The world often views 'success' and popularity differently than how God sees. What's at the heart? Eventually, the truth of who they are will be brought into the light.

> *"Therefore judge nothing before the time, until the Lord come, who both will bring to light the hidden things of darkness, and will make manifest the counsels of the hearts: and then shall every man have praise of God."*
> 1 Corinthians 4:5

We can trust His word to be true and rely on Him for guiding us.

3. Know God's word and you'll know when it's being twisted and manipulated.

> *"And no marvel; for Satan himself is transformed into an angel of light. Therefore it is no great thing if his ministers also be transformed as the ministers of righteousness; whose end shall be according to their works."* 2 Corinthians 11:14-15

Sometimes deception may be hidden well, manipulated and cunning, for the Bible makes clear that even satan disguises himself as light. If we don't know His truth, we will never know when we're being deceived. Study it. Meditate on His words. Guard them in your heart. *"Thy word have I hid in mine heart, that I might not sin against thee."* Psalm 119:11

Press in close to God. Spend time in His presence. Pray, talk with God, listen to His voice through His word. Staying close to His side, living under the protection of His armour and covering, helps us to know when we're staring straight into falsehood.

4. Trust the discernment and wisdom of God's Spirit living through your life.

"...Then if any man shall say unto you, Lo, here is Christ, or there; believe it not. For there shall arise false Christs, and false prophets, and shall shew great signs and wonders; insomuch that, if it were possible, they shall deceive the very elect. Behold, I have told you before." Matthew 24:23-25

God gives us His Spirit to guide us in discernment and wisdom.

"Howbeit when he, the Spirit of truth, is come, he will guide you into all the truth..." John 16:13

He wants more than anyone, for us to be guided in Truth. He tells us "I have told you ahead of time," so that we will be prepared and watching. Walking in the Spirit and not in the flesh. We don't have to wander through life blindly, unsure of what's true and what's not. When we're daily asking for his leadership and direction, submitting to his authority over our lives, we can trust the leadership of His Spirit. When feeling unsettled or sensing something is just not 'quite right,' we can press in close to Him, knowing He's faithful to guide us.

5. Surround yourself with other believers you know and trust.

"Knowing this...there shall come in the last days with scoffing, walking after their own lusts." 2 Peter 3:3

Use caution in who you listen to and choose to take guidance from. Sometimes when we're in a place where it's hard to see clearly, maybe because of our own pressing worries or cares, we need a trusted friend who can speak truth in places we need to hear. This is often true in marriage. Learning to listen to one another and take into consideration what the other might be sensing or discerning can often have great power in saving us from a heap of trouble up ahead, if we'll only heed the warnings that someone we love may speak our way.

> "*Where no counsel is, the people fall: but in the multitude of counsellors there is safety.*" Proverbs 11:14

Recognize that sometimes believers may simply disagree. It doesn't necessarily mean that one is a "false teacher," but only that both might be doing their best to follow God's Word and what He's leading, they just may not agree on everything. We see this in Scripture, and we see it all around us today.

Let's not waste time fighting against ourselves but recognize who the real enemy is. We can choose to give each other grace and kindness. We can hold on to what matters most and pursue unity in the body of Christ.

Standing strong together, on Christ the Solid Rock. Although many believe that the "fruits" spoken of here must be "good works", I believe that the verses immediately following these ones make it clear that this cannot be the case.

> "*Not every one that saith unto me, Lord, Lord, shall enter into the kingdom of heaven; but he that doeth the will of my Father which is in heaven. Many will say to me in that day, Lord, Lord, have we not prophesied in thy name? and in thy name have cast out devils? and in*

thy name done many wonderful works?_And then will I profess unto them, I never knew you: depart from me, ye that work iniquity." Matthew 7:21-23

The people who are told to 'depart' by Jesus, brought Him their 'many wonderful works' which they had done in His name. The reason He told them He never knew them is because 'wonderful works' are not what gets us into Heaven. Only faith in the finished work of Christ, the Gospel, can do so. (As only those who do the will of the Father, which is to believe in the Son, will enter the Kingdom of Heaven).

So, if the 'good fruits' spoken of are not 'good works', what are they? I believe that the 'fruits' spoken of are teachings, or doctrine. After all, what are prophets known for? They are known for speaking truth from God, either warning or encouraging those who listen in the ways of the Lord, by communicating messages from Him. (The most important being the Gospel of our Salvation).

To quote Reinhard Bonnke: "The need in Africa, India, Pakistan and the rest of the world is not the call. This piece of wisdom has saved the lives of many a missionary, especially in Africa, where the needs are so great that they can pull you to pieces. A missionary can put out so many fires trying to meet needs around him that he suffers burnout. I have known missionary friends who said, 'I hear the cry of lost souls calling me into the mission field.' These workers are headed for the missionary bone yard. They have responded to the call of the need rather than the call of God."

"We must go where God sends us, speak what He gives us to speak, hear His voice and obey it — this is our best protection from burnout. It will also guide us to the very best strategy for accomplishing His mission. For everything a man does to follow the call of God, there are ten things he does not do. We cannot do everything. We must focus on the call and not simply the need." (Living a Life of Fire Copyright @ 2010 Inc)

Regrets makes a very poor companion

We all have thorns – those things that rise up around us, strangling us. Thorns don't keep a seed from sprouting but they will keep it from producing fruit. We all make bad decisions sometimes. Cut that thorn away and see how God nourishes your life.

God knows my name. I have a call on my life, and I am here for a divine purpose. I am a Gentile, but I have Royal Blood in me through the cross; when things come against me. When hell comes against my marriage, my family, my friends, my finances – I plead the Blood because it is the precious Blood of Jesus Christ which brings strength; it brings protection!

God has and is still doing mighty things in my life so I ask you, who can know what God will ever do with one life totally sold out for Him? Regrets, I have a few but God will restore the years the locusts have eaten of that I have no doubts and am humbled that He chose me to serve in the teaching and preaching ministry internationally.

My closing thoughts: The rest of my years will be the best of my years. God is not finished with me yet. I ask God to replenish me with living water every day of my life. Some of us quit too easily and too soon! For me, I am blessed and not depressed; I am anointed and not disappointed. I have everything in Christ.

Lord; I present my body a living sacrifice to you. Anoint my eyes to see souls perishing. Anoint my ears not to be trash containers. Anoint my mind and renew it that I will walk and do right. In the mighty name of Jesus Christ, I pray, Amen.